REVISE PEARSON EDEXCEL GCSE (9–1)
Religious Studies B: Christianity and Islam

MODEL ANSWER WORKBOOK

Series Consultant: Harry Smith

Author: Tanya Hill

T0346309

Also available to support your revision:

Revise GCSE Study Skills Guide   9781292318875

The **Revise GCSE Study Skills Guide** is full of tried-and-trusted hints and tips for how to learn more effectively. It gives you techniques to help you achieve your best – throughout your GCSE studies and beyond!

Revise GCSE Revision Planner   9781292318868

The **Revise GCSE Revision Planner** helps you to plan and organise your time, step-by-step, throughout your GCSE revision. Use this book and wall chart to mastermind your revision.

For the full range of Pearson Edexcel revision titles across KS2, KS3, GCSE, Functional Skills, AS/A Level and BTEC visit: www.pearsonschools.co.uk/revise

Contents

A small bit of small print:

Pearson Edexcel publishes Sample Assessment Material and the Specification on its website. This is the official content and this book should be used in conjunction with it. The questions and mark schemes have been written to help you practise every topic in the book. Remember: the real exam questions and mark schemes may not look like this.

About your exam

Your Pearson Edexcel (9–1) Religious Studies B GCSE consists of **three** Areas of Study, from which you must choose and study **two** that are then assessed through two examinations. The studied religion must be different for each Area of Study chosen.

Paper 1

Area of Study 1 – Religion and Ethics

Students must study all four content sections based upon their chosen religion:

- Beliefs
- Marriage and the Family
- Living the Religious Life
- Matters of Life and Death.

The paper is:

 written   1 hour 45 minutes    worth 102 marks   50% of the total.

Paper 2

Area of Study 2 – Religion, Peace and Conflict

Students must study all four content sections based upon their chosen religion:

- Beliefs
- Crime and Punishment
- Living the Religious Life
- Peace and Conflict.

The paper is:

 written   1 hour 45 minutes   worth 102 marks   50% of the total.

Paper 3

Area of Study 3 – Religion, Philosophy and Social Justice

Students must study all four content sections based upon their chosen religion:

- Beliefs
- Philosophy of Religion
- Living the Religious Life
- Equality.

The paper is:

 written   1 hour 45 minutes   worth 102 marks   50% of the total.

Each paper will assess spelling, punctuation and grammar (SPaG) and use of specialist terminology, which will contribute a minimum of 5% of marks towards the overall score.

9   8   7   6   5   4   3   2   1   U

Command words and mark schemes

Understanding command words

A command word tells you how you should answer a question. Here is an introduction to the most common command words used in the Pearson Edexcel (9–1) Religious Studies B GCSE and some tips on how to answer questions that use them.

State / Outline
Provide knowledge of religion and belief by recalling or listing factual information. You are required to give three different points. Don't try to develop ideas or explain them – just state what they are.

Explain
Provide knowledge and understanding of an aspect of religion and belief by stating an idea and then developing it by adding further information, an example or a religious teaching. You should make sure your ideas are different (not repeated) and clearly linked to the question.

Evaluate
Interpret a statement to consider different viewpoints. Include logical reasoning and make connections between elements of the question. End with a justified conclusion. Address all elements of the question (using the bullet points) and consider arguments that both agree and disagree with the statement.

Describe
Provide knowledge through a comparison between Christianity or Islam and another religion you have studied. This type of question can only be asked for the topics: *Beliefs about the afterlife and their significance* (Topics 1.6 Christianity / 1.8 Islam) and *The practice and significance of worship* (Topics 3.1 Christianity / 3.3 Islam).

Explain *with reference to a source of wisdom and authority*
Provide knowledge and understanding of an aspect of religion and belief by stating an idea and then developing it by adding further information, an example or a religious teaching. In addition, there must be a reference to a source of religious authority, for example by quoting or paraphrasing from a holy book.

Understanding mark schemes

Mark schemes tell you what the marker is looking for in your answer; they do not necessarily include every possible answer you could write. Throughout this book, you will be introduced to mark schemes alongside exam-style answers. Here are some things to look out for:

The bullet points tell you what types of answers are acceptable.

Mark schemes for short answer questions

Question	Answer
1 AO1 3 marks	Award one mark for each point. • Christians believe death is not the end. (1) • The resurrection of Jesus is evidence. (1)

Extended answers are given a level first. Then, to award a mark, you need to decide whether the answer is at the top or the bottom end of that level.

Mark scheme for extended answer questions

The descriptors are a guide to the features that an answer must include to achieve each level. At the top of a level, an answer will include all of the descriptors. At the bottom of a level, an answer will include at least one of the descriptors and usually all of the ones from the level below.

Level	Descriptor
4 10–12 marks	• Clear understanding of the skill of evaluation is demonstrated with knowledge around the issues used to support judgements made. • The strengths and weaknesses of arguments are considered. • A summary conclusion is offered which justifies which is the stronger side of the argument, with supporting evidence.
3 7–9 marks	• Good understanding of the demands of the question with some, but not all, elements of the question being considered. • Arguments are used on both sides of the debate with good use of knowledge and sources of authority to support. • A reasoned conclusion is offered with some evidence but lacks some strength in justification.

How to use this book

In this book, you will familiarise yourself with the Pearson Edexcel (9–1) Religious Studies B GCSE by engaging with exam-style questions, answers and mark schemes. Doing so will mean you know exactly what to expect in the exam and, just as importantly, what will be expected of you.

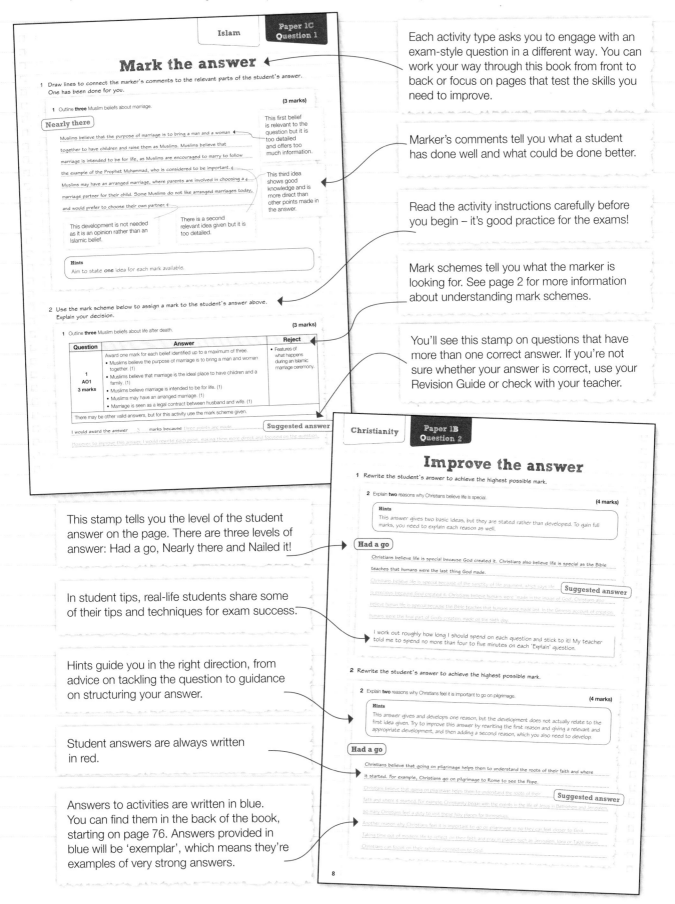

Each activity type asks you to engage with an exam-style question in a different way. You can work your way through this book from front to back or focus on pages that test the skills you need to improve.

Marker's comments tell you what a student has done well and what could be done better.

Read the activity instructions carefully before you begin – it's good practice for the exams!

Mark schemes tell you what the marker is looking for. See page 2 for more information about understanding mark schemes.

You'll see this stamp on questions that have more than one correct answer. If you're not sure whether your answer is correct, use your Revision Guide or check with your teacher.

This stamp tells you the level of the student answer on the page. There are three levels of answer: Had a go, Nearly there and Nailed it!

In student tips, real-life students share some of their tips and techniques for exam success.

Hints guide you in the right direction, from advice on tackling the question to guidance on structuring your answer.

Student answers are always written in red.

Answers to activities are written in blue. You can find them in the back of the book, starting on page 76. Answers provided in blue will be 'exemplar', which means they're examples of very strong answers.

Mark the answer

1 Draw lines to connect the marker's comments to the relevant parts of the student's answer. One has been done for you.

---

1 Outline **three** Christian beliefs about how the biblical account of creation should be understood. **(3 marks)**

> **Hints**
>
> When answering 3-mark 'Outline' questions, state each idea you present in a separate and distinct sentence, as this will make your three ideas clear to the examiner.

All Christians believe that God created the universe and everything in it, as Genesis states. Some Christians believe the Genesis account of creation in the Bible is literally true. Other Christians may take a more mythical interpretation, believing the biblical account explains why the world was created rather than how.

The student begins their answer with a clear statement to show they understand the key belief all Christians hold about the creation account in the Bible.

The student shows they understand a less literal way in which the account can be understood.

A second belief is stated, showing how some Christians read the creation account literally, believing only what is said in Genesis.

---

2 Draw lines to connect the marker's comments to the relevant parts of the student's answer. One has been done for you.

---

1 Outline **three** Christian beliefs about divorce. **(3 marks)**

Christians believe marriage should be for life. Christians believe the Bible teaches 'what God has joined together, let no one separate'. Christians believe they make promises for life in the marriage ceremony.

This idea is correct but repeats the first idea given in the answer.

The second part of this answer gives a clear teaching from the Bible to outline a Christian belief.

Although a relevant idea has been stated, the link to divorce could be made clearer by stating that Christians do not encourage divorce because they believe marriage should be for life.

If the question says 'state' or 'outline', I'm careful not to expand on points to explain them. I don't want to do more than I need to in the exam – it will only waste valuable time!

Mark the answer

1 Use the mark scheme to decide to which of the answers below you would **not** award full marks. Explain your choice.

1 Outline **three** Christian beliefs about life after death. **(3 marks)**

Question	Answer	Reject
1 **AO1** **3 marks**	Award one mark for each belief identified up to a maximum of three. • Christians believe death is not the end. (1) • The resurrection of Jesus is evidence of life after death for Christians. (1) • Christians believe in heaven and hell. (1) • Christians believe God will judge humans after death. (1) • Christians believe those who believe in God will go to heaven. (1)	• Christians do not believe in life after death. • Christians believe in reincarnation.
There may be other valid answers, but for this activity use the mark scheme given.		

I take a minute to read the question carefully, to make sure I understand what it is asking me to do.

Hints

You need to be direct when answering this style of question – aim to give one idea in each sentence.

A
Christians believe that there is an afterlife.
Christians believe humans who deserve reward will go to heaven after death.
Christians believe God judges humans after death.

B
Christians believe there are two places after death. One is heaven and the other is hell.

Answer .... would not get full marks because ....

....

....

Complete the answer

1 Complete the student's answer so that it would be awarded 3 marks.

---

1 Outline **three** Christian beliefs about the importance of the incarnation. **(3 marks)**

> **Hints**
>
> Two beliefs have been given in this answer. The question asks you to outline three beliefs, so you need to add one more.

Nearly there

The incarnation is important as it helps Christians to understand what God is like. Christians believe that

Jesus as human is important because he showed them how they should behave in their lives.

....

....

> I work out roughly how much time I have for each style of question and try to stick to it. So for 3-mark 'Outline' questions I aim to complete my answer within three minutes, which means I have one minute to write down each of the three points I need to make.

---

2 Complete the student's answer so that it would be awarded 3 marks.

---

1 Outline **three** reasons why Christians believe they should care for the world. **(3 marks)**

> **Hints**
>
> This time, only one reason has been given, so you need to add two more relevant reasons.

Had a go

Christians accept that, as God created the world, they have a responsibility to care for it.

....

....

Complete the answer

1 Complete the student's answer so that it would be awarded 4 marks.

2 Explain **two** reasons why the biblical account of creation is important for Christians today. **(4 marks)**

> **Hints**
> Each of the two reasons given below will gain 1 mark. To gain full marks, each reason needs development. This could be done by adding another sentence of information, an example or a religious teaching.

Nearly there

The story of creation in the Bible is important to Christians today because it confirms their belief that God

created the universe and everything in it.

....

Nearly there

It is important because it helps Christians to understand why the world was created.

....

....

2 Complete the student's answer so that it would be awarded 4 marks.

2 Explain **two** reasons why the existence of evil and suffering in the world challenges the nature of God. **(4 marks)**

> **Hints**
> Make sure that the explanation you give is specific to the nature (characteristics) of God.

Nearly there

Evil and suffering in the world may challenge the Christian belief in God as omnipotent.

....

....

Evil and suffering may also challenge the Christian belief in God as benevolent.

....

....

I created flash cards to help me learn key words when revising, so I could use them
accurately in my answers.

Improve the answer

1 Rewrite the student's answer to achieve the highest possible mark.

2 Explain **two** reasons why Christians believe life is special. **(4 marks)**

Hints

This answer gives two basic ideas, but they are stated rather than developed. To gain full marks, you need to explain each reason as well.

Had a go

Christians believe life is special because God created it. Christians also believe life is special as the Bible teaches that humans were the last thing God made.

....

....

....

....

I work out roughly how long I should spend on each question and stick to it! My teacher told me to spend no more than four to five minutes on each 'Explain' question.

2 Rewrite the student's answer to achieve the highest possible mark.

2 Explain **two** reasons why Christians feel it is important to go on pilgrimage. **(4 marks)**

Hints

This answer gives and develops one reason, but the development does not actually relate to the first idea given. Try to improve this answer by rewriting the first reason and giving a relevant and appropriate development, and then adding a second reason, which you also need to develop.

Had a go

Christians believe that going on pilgrimage helps them to understand the roots of their faith and where it started. For example, Christians go on pilgrimage to Rome to see the Pope.

....

....

....

....

....

....

Mark the answer

1 Draw lines to connect the marker's comments to the relevant parts of the student's answer. One has been done for you.

2 Explain **two** reasons why the resurrection of Jesus is important to Christians.

(4 marks)

Nearly there

The resurrection of Jesus is important to Christians as it demonstrates the

Christian belief in life after death. Christians live their lives following the Bible

teaching that states they can achieve eternal life in heaven with God if they follow

the example of Jesus. The resurrection of Jesus is also important, as it provides

evidence to support the Christian belief in Jesus as the Son of God.

This sentence gives a first relevant reason why the resurrection of Jesus is important to Christians.

This sentence develops the first reason given by adding further explanation.

I always try to think about both the reasons I intend to put in my answer before I start writing, to make sure I'm not just saying the same thing in two different ways.

This sentence gives a second relevant reason why the resurrection of Jesus is important to Christians. It now needs to be developed further.

2 Now use the mark scheme below to decide how many marks you would award the student's answer.

Question	Answer	Reject
2 **AO1** **4 marks**	Award one mark for providing each reason and one mark for developing each reason. Up to a maximum of four marks. • It shows belief in life after death. (1) It gives hope that if they follow biblical teachings, they will achieve heaven. (1) • It proves Jesus was the Son of God. (1) It supports the idea that Christians should follow Jesus as he came to earth as God in human form (incarnation). (1) • It reminds Christians of the power of God over life and death. (1) Jesus' death and resurrection shows God decides when a person lives or dies and shows life is special. (1)	• Repeated reason / development. • Development that does not relate both to the reason given and to the question.
There may be other valid answers, but for this activity use the mark scheme given.		

I would award the answer .... marks because ....

....

....

....

Mark the answer

1 Draw lines to connect the marker's comments to the relevant parts of the student's answer. One has been done for you.

> 3 Explain **two** ways the Trinity is reflected in Christian worship.
>
> In your answer you must refer to a source of wisdom and authority. **(5 marks)**
>
> **Nearly there**
>
> The Trinity can be seen when Christians worship through the way they bless
>
> themselves. They make the sign of the cross, representing the idea of the Father,
>
> the Son and the Holy Spirit. The Trinity is also part of many prayers or creeds
>
> spoken by Christians. Prayers and creeds may refer to God as the 'maker of heaven
>
> and Earth', showing the beliefs of the Trinity are important to Christians.

The student has identified one way in which the Trinity is seen in Christian worship.

Sources of Christian wisdom and authority are referred to, and a quote is used.

This is developed well: specific information about the sign of the cross is given.

This statement does not answer the question and is irrelevant.

The student has identified a second way.

> It helped me to think about how my answers would be marked when I was revising. Using this technique improved my confidence with exam questions.

2 Now use the mark scheme below to decide how many marks you would award the student's answer.

Question	Answer
3 **AO1** **5 marks**	Award one mark for each way and one mark for developing each way. Up to a maximum of four marks. Award one further mark for any relevant source of wisdom and authority. • The Trinity is seen in worship when Christians bless themselves. (1) They 'make the sign of the cross'. (1) They speak the words of the Trinity ('in the name of the Father, the Son and the Holy Spirit'). (1) • The Trinity is used in worship as part of many prayers. (1) The Lord's Prayer is an example. (1) 'Our Father in Heaven, hallowed be your name' (Matthew 6:9) refers to God as part of the Trinity. (1) • The Trinity is part of Christian creeds in services of worship. (1) The Nicene Creed contains key beliefs about the Trinity. (1) The Nicene Creed contains the words 'for us and our salvation, he came down from heaven'. (1)
There may be other valid answers, but for this activity use the mark scheme given.	

I would award the answer .... marks because ....

....

....

....

....

Improve the answer

1 Rewrite the student's answer to achieve the highest possible mark.

3 Explain **two** reasons why many Christians do not accept abortion.

In your answer you must refer to a source of wisdom and authority. **(5 marks)**

Had a go

Many Christians do not accept abortion because they support the sanctity of life argument.

Another reason is that Christians believe life starts at conception and so they view abortion as murder.

However, there are some cases (for example, rape) where some Christians believe abortion may be seen

as acceptable.

Hints
- Some good reasons are included in this answer, but they are not developed.
- As well as identifying and developing two different reasons, you need to link at least one of your reasons to a relevant source of authority for Christians – for example, by including a quote or putting a teaching in your own words (paraphrasing).
- The question asks for two reasons why Christians do not accept abortion, so do not include any reasons why they may support it.

....

....

....

....

....

....

....

Complete the answer

1 Complete the student's answer so that it would be awarded 5 marks.

3 Explain **two** reasons why the family is considered important to Christians today.

In your answer you must refer to a source of wisdom and authority. **(5 marks)**

Had a go

Many Christians believe the family is important today, as they accept it was God's intention for humanity.

Many Christians see the family unit as providing stability and security for children while they grow up within

the Christian faith.

....

....

....

....

I was really worried about having to learn quotes from religious texts for my exam, but my teacher told me just to learn a few short phrases and then think about how I could summarise longer quotes in my own words. This approach made revision so much easier and really helped me to recall the information when I needed it in the exam.

2 Complete the student's answer so that it would be awarded 5 marks.

3 Explain **two** reasons why some Christians may prefer liturgical worship.

In your answer you must refer to a source of wisdom and authority. **(5 marks)**

Had a go

Some Christians may belong to a denomination where liturgical worship, such as taking part in the Eucharist

service, plays an important role.

Liturgical worship may give Christians a sense of belonging as they carry out set patterns in their worship

with other Christians.

....

....

....

....

....

....

Mark the answer

Draw lines to connect the marker's comments to the relevant parts of the student's answer. One has been done for you.

4 "Easter is the most important festival for Christians to celebrate."

Evaluate this statement considering arguments for and against.

In your response you should:

- refer to Christian teachings
- refer to different Christian points of view
- reach a justified conclusion.

(15 marks)

Nearly there

Some Christians may agree with the statement because Easter celebrates the resurrection of Jesus, which supports belief in the afterlife. In the Bible, the Book of John teaches that those who believe in Jesus will achieve eternal life, reinforcing Easter's importance. Many Christians spend a lot of time reflecting on the importance of the afterlife and how best to follow Jesus' teachings to achieve a place in heaven, and celebrating Easter is a key part of how they do this. Christians believe Jesus was God in human form and that he died to redeem humanity's sins. This suggests Easter is important because it recalls a key event of significance in the religion. These are strong arguments that many Christians would support, as they reflect Bible teachings concerning God, life after death and the role of Jesus.

On the other hand, some Christians argue that the festival of Christmas is more important than Easter, as it celebrates Jesus' birth. This shows the importance of God's message to the world – God so loved the world that he sent his only son to be born on earth that we may know his love. While I don't feel this is the strongest argument, I do think that many Christians prefer celebrating Christmas, as it is a happy time of year that brings people together and is celebrated globally. Prophets in the Bible predicted the birth of Jesus as the Messiah and Son of God, so Christmas could be seen as more important because it shows God's power in the way the prophecies of Jesus' birth came true.

Overall, therefore, I do not agree with the statement. While Christians recognise Easter as an important festival, it is not necessarily the most important one. For many Christians, all elements and beliefs of Christian worship are equally important, so I do not feel that celebrating Easter is more important than celebrating any other festival in the religion.

The reasons given to agree are developed, with relevant knowledge and reference to Christian teachings. The student has used them consistently and accurately.

There is a change of argument here with a reason to disagree with the statement. Further reasons may add more value to this part of the answer.

The answer begins well with a direct link to the question, giving a number of reasons why a Christian may agree with the statement.

The answer finishes strongly with a justified conclusion. The student has been careful not simply to repeat their arguments; instead, they have successfully summarised their evaluation.

Once the reasons have been stated and developed, this answer successfully evaluates the strength of the reasons.

Reorder the answer

1 Rearrange the paragraphs into the most logical order by numbering each part of the student's answer.

4 "The resurrection is the most important event in the life of Jesus."

Evaluate this statement considering arguments for and against.

In your response you should:

- refer to Christian teachings
- refer to different Christian points of view
- reach a justified conclusion.

(15 marks)

☐ A final reason why some Christians may agree is that the resurrection of Jesus offers Christians hope. Christians believe that God sent Jesus to earth to die to forgive the sins of humanity. Through the resurrection of Jesus, Christians learn not to fear death. They understand that humans will be offered salvation and that Jesus' death made this possible.

☐ In conclusion, Christians hold different views about this statement – all of which are equally valid. I feel the strongest reason is that no 'one' event in the life of Jesus is more important than any other, as they are all equally significant. Jesus as the Son of God holds a special place of importance for Christians, and it is through understanding all the events in Jesus' life that Christians believe they can get closer to God.

☐ Other Christians, however, may disagree with the statement. They may argue that all the events in the life of Jesus – including his resurrection – are important. All events in Jesus' life offer proof that he was the Son of God, including his birth, his teachings and his ability to perform miracles.

☐ Some Christians may agree with the statement because they believe that the resurrection of Jesus is proof of an afterlife. It shows Christians that death is not the end and that they can follow the example of Jesus and be rewarded in heaven if they live as God intends. The Bible says that those who believe in Jesus will gain eternal life.

☐ Furthermore, some Christians may believe that other events are more important than the resurrection of Jesus. His death through crucifixion shows the sacrifice he made so that God would forgive humanity's sins.

☐ Another reason why Christians may agree with the statement is because the resurrection proves Jesus is the Son of God and reinforces Christian belief in the Trinity (Father, Son and Holy Spirit). Christians refer to the Trinity in their prayers (for example, the Lord's Prayer) and it is a central part of their worship.

Organising my answer is important to me as it helps me to include the required elements. I find that checking off the bulleted list in the question is a good way of making sure I have all the parts needed in my answer.

The 15-mark 'Evaluate' questions, have 3 marks available for SPaG. For those questions, I always made sure I left a couple of minutes to check my answer thoroughly for spelling, punctuation and grammar, and to ensure I had used some specialist terms in my answer.

Improve the answer

1 Write an improved answer to the question below. Use the hints to make sure your answer achieves the highest possible mark.

---

4 "The resurrection is the most important event in the life of Jesus."

Evaluate this statement considering arguments for and against. In your response you should:

- refer to Christian teachings
- refer to different Christian points of view
- reach a justified conclusion.

(15 marks)

Had a go

Some Christians may agree with this statement because they accept the resurrection of Jesus as proof of an afterlife. They may also believe that the resurrection of Jesus shows he is special and that he really is the Son of God. However, other Christians may believe that all the events in the life of Jesus are equally important, as they show he was the Son of God. Some Christians may also believe that the crucifixion is the most important event, as it shows the sacrifice God was willing to make. I feel that the strongest argument is that it is Jesus himself who is important – including all the events of his life. No single event, such as the resurrection, is more important than the others.

Find the answer

1 Using the marking instructions below, which **one** of the four points would you **not** include in your answer to the following question? Explain your choice. Then explain why you would include the other three points.

---

1 Outline **three** beliefs about Zakah for Muslims. **(3 marks)**

Marking instructions
Award one mark for each point identified up to a maximum of three.

A | Muslims believe Zakah is a duty for all Muslims to give to charity.

B | Muslims believe the Qur'an teaches them that Zakah is commanded by Allah.

C | Some Muslims will also give Khums as well as Zakah.

D | Muslims believe that Zakah helps to support all Muslims in the ummah.

> **Hints**
> Make sure your responses are direct and linked to the question being asked.

I would not include point .... because ....

....

....

I would include points .... because ....

....

Mark the answer

1 Draw lines to connect the marker's comments to the relevant parts of the student's answer. One has been done for you.

1 Outline **three** Muslim beliefs about marriage. **(3 marks)**

Nearly there

Muslims believe that the purpose of marriage is to bring a man and a woman ◄

together to have children and raise them as Muslims. Muslims believe that

marriage is intended to be for life, as Muslims are encouraged to marry to follow

the example of the Prophet Muhammad, who is considered to be important.

Muslims may have an arranged marriage, where parents are involved in choosing a

marriage partner for their child. Some Muslims do not like arranged marriages today,

and would prefer to choose their own partner.

This first belief is relevant to the question but it is too detailed and offers too much information.

This third idea shows good knowledge and is more direct than other points made in the answer.

This development is not needed as it is an opinion rather than an Islamic belief.

There is a second relevant idea given but it is too detailed.

Hints

Aim to state **one** idea for each mark available.

2 Use the mark scheme below to assign a mark to the student's answer above. Explain your decision.

1 Outline **three** Muslim beliefs about life after death. **(3 marks)**

Question	Answer	Reject
1 **AO1** **3 marks**	Award one mark for each belief identified up to a maximum of three. • Muslims believe the purpose of marriage is to bring a man and woman together. (1) • Muslims believe that marriage is the ideal place to have children and a family. (1) • Muslims believe marriage is intended to be for life. (1) • Muslims may have an arranged marriage. (1) • Marriage is seen as a legal contract between husband and wife. (1)	• Features of what happens during an Islamic marriage ceremony.
There may be other valid answers, but for this activity use the mark scheme given.		

I would award the answer .... marks because ....

....

Complete the answer

1 Complete the student's answer so that it would be awarded 3 marks.

---

1 Outline **three** ways the Muslim community provides support for families.   **(3 marks)**

> **Hints**
>
> One way in which Muslims provide support for families in their local area is given below. You need to add two more ways.

Had a go

Muslims may provide classes for parents to attend.

....

....

> I always have a go at answering a question, even if I'm not completely sure of the answer. I will definitely score 0 for no answer, so I figure it's better to write something down and give myself the chance of gaining some marks.

---

2 Complete the student's answer so that it would be awarded 3 marks.

---

1 Outline **three** reasons why Muslims do not accept euthanasia.   **(3 marks)**

> **Hints**
>
> You could state a religious teaching in your answer. You can do this either by quoting it directly (using speech marks to show it is a quotation) or by paraphrasing (putting it in your own words).

Had a go

Muslims do not accept euthanasia as they believe only Allah can decide when a person should die.

....

....

Mark the answer

1 Use the mark scheme to decide to which of these student answers you would not award
full marks. Explain your choice.

2 Explain **two** reasons why the characteristics of Allah are important for Muslims today. **(4 marks)**

Question	Answer	Reject
2 **AO1** **4 marks**	Award one mark for each reason identified up to a maximum of three. • They help Muslims to understand Allah better. (1) Muslims believe that they spend their lives in submission to Allah, so understanding what he is like helps to strengthen their relationship with him. (1) • Muslims believe that the characteristics of Allah help them to follow how he wants them to live their lives. (1) Muslims believe that just as Allah is forgiving, they should also try to be forgiving towards others. (1) • Muslims believe understanding what Allah is like will help them to be good Muslims. (1) Understanding that Allah is a judge who will decide their afterlife is important in making sure they will achieve paradise. (1)	• Repeated reason/development. • Development that does not relate both to the reason given and to the question.

There may be other valid answers, but for this activity use the mark scheme given.

A The characteristics of Allah help Muslims to develop a relationship with him. An important part of being a Muslim is submission to Allah, and understanding what he is like will allow Muslims to do this. Muslims also live their lives trying to please Allah, so they will be rewarded in the afterlife. Muslims believe that understanding Allah's characteristics will allow them to live their lives as he intended.

B Muslims believe Allah is omnipotent, which means he is all-powerful. This can be seen in the way he created the universe and everything within it.
Muslims also believe Allah is a judge who will decide their afterlife. He will judge them after death.

C Muslims believe that everything they do should show submission to Allah, so understanding how Allah wants them to live is important. For example, knowing that Allah is forgiving teaches Muslims that they should try to be forgiving towards others too.
Knowing Allah's characteristics also helps Muslims to develop a relationship with him. Muslims want to be rewarded in paradise after death, so knowing that Allah will judge them on their actions in this life guides them to live a good life so they can achieve paradise.

Answer .... would **not** get full marks because ....

....

....

Mark the answer

1 Use the mark scheme below to assign a mark to the student's answer. Explain your decision.

2 Explain **two** Muslim teachings about gender equality.

(4 marks)

Had a go

Islam teaches that Allah created all humans – both male and female. Islam teaches that men and women will be

treated in the same way after death in the afterlife, showing they are equal.

Question	Answer	Reject
2 **AO1** **4 marks**	Award one mark for each teaching and one mark for developing each teaching. Up to a maximum of four marks. • Islam teaches that Allah created all humans – both male and female. (1) While Allah created different roles for men and women (men to provide, women to care for the home and children), these roles are seen to complement each other and be equal. (1) • Islam teaches that Allah will judge men and women in the same way after death. (1) Surah 33:35 talks about Allah judging men and women in the same way for their actions and beliefs after death. (1) • Islam teaches that men and women are given the same religious responsibilities from Allah, showing equality. (1) For example, both men and women are expected to pray five times a day, and to marry and have a family to please Allah. (1)	• Repeated teaching/development. • Development that does not relate both to the teaching given and to the question.
There may be other valid answers, but for this activity use the mark scheme given.		

I would award the answer   marks because

....

....

....

....

Complete the answer

1 Complete the student's answer so that it would be awarded 4 marks.

> **2** Explain **two** reasons why completing Hajj is important for Muslims.   **(4 marks)**
>
> **Hints**
>
> Two reasons have been stated. This question asks you to 'explain' each reason, so you now need to add supporting detail to each reason to get full marks.

Nearly there

Muslims believe completing Hajj is important as it is one of the Five Pillars of Islam, which are a duty for all Muslims.

....

Nearly there

Muslims also believe Hajj is important as it strengthens their ummah and individual faith.

....

....

2 Complete the student's answer so that it would be awarded 4 marks.

> **2** Explain **two** reasons why Muslims try to look after Allah's creation in the way he wants them to.   **(4 marks)**
>
> **Hints**
>
> For 4-mark 'Explain' questions, two reasons need to be stated and each reason needs to be developed with further information. In this example, the development of each reason is given and you need to identify the reasons that have been developed.

....

....

Nearly there   The Hadith teaches Muslims that 'the earth is green and beautiful and Allah has appointed you stewards over it'.

....

Nearly there   Muslims believe that, after death, Allah will judge them and they will have to answer for how they have cared for his creation.

> I always think about how I will develop each idea before choosing what to write, as sometimes I have an idea but can't successfully develop it.

Find the answer

1 A student has planned an answer to the question below. Find:

- one point that is **not** accurate

- one point that is **not** relevant.

Explain your choices.

---

3 Explain **two** reasons why some Muslims accept the use of contraception.

In your answer you must refer to a source of wisdom and authority. **(5 marks)**

> **Hints**
>
> You will only gain marks for information that is accurate and relevant in your answers.

A   Some Muslims believe that it is acceptable to use contraception if the mother's life may be at risk.

B   Muslims believe in the sanctity of life (which says all life is sacred) and so, if the mother and other children will be affected by another pregnancy, using contraception may be preferable.

C   Some Muslims believe family planning is sensible.

D   Muslims believe they should plan when to have their families around their careers.

E   Some Hadith accounts (e.g. Sahih al-Bukhari) seem to suggest that Muhammad spoke out against the use of natural contraception and did not support it.

The information that I think is not accurate is   because
....
....

The information that I think is not relevant to this question is   because
....
....

Improve the answer

1 A student has written an answer to this question. Use the hints below to improve it.

---

3 Explain **two** reasons why prophets are important in Islam.

In your answer you must refer to a source of wisdom and authority. **(5 marks)**

> **Hints**
> - So far, this student's answer simply states two reasons. You need to focus on explaining each reason.
> - Make sure you include a teaching from a source of wisdom or authority that is relevant to the question and explain what it means.

Had a go

Prophets are important because Allah uses them to communicate with humanity. Prophets are also important because they have brought holy books to the world. The Qur'an has many teachings about the importance of prophets.

....

....

....

....

....

....

....

I found it really hard to learn quotes for the exam. Then I realised that as long as I understand the quote's meaning, I can paraphrase it in my own words. I still have to check my work carefully though, so I can link the quotes to what the question is asking.

Mark the answer

1 Draw lines to connect the marker's comments to the relevant parts of the student's answer.
   One has been done for you.

3 Explain **two** reasons why belief in Tawhid is important to Muslims.

In your answer you must refer to a source of wisdom and authority.   **(5 marks)**

> **Hints**
>
> - In this answer, several ideas are given – but the student could have provided less information and still gained the full 5 marks, saving time in the exam.
> - No extra marks would be awarded for the inclusion of a second quotation, as the question only requires a link to one source of wisdom and authority.
> - Remember that you will save time (which can be allocated to other questions) by keeping your answers concise.

Nailed it!

Tawhid is considered one of the most important beliefs in Islam because it sums up the essential truth that Muslims believe in one God. This belief unites and is shared by all Muslims in the ummah, and is reinforced by the Qur'an and through speaking the Shahadah. The Qur'an teaches Muslims in Surah 16 to 'worship Allah and avoid Taghut', meaning that they should only worship one God – Allah. Another reason why belief in Tawhid is important to Muslims is because it underpins all other beliefs in the religion. Muslims believe they have to submit to Allah in all parts of their lives – for example, by praying five times a day and by completing Hajj, Sawm and Zakah – and that by doing so they are respecting belief in Tawhid. As Surah 112 states, 'He is Allah'; this shows that acceptance of Tawhid is important.

The second reason given in this answer is clear, different to the first reason and stated directly.

This quote about worshipping Allah provides a link to a source of wisdom and authority (required by the question). The quote is relevant and the student has successfully linked it to the reason given.

The second reason is developed in the same way as the first, with the addition of further information – in this case, examples.

The answer finishes by making a link to a second relevant quote from the Qur'an. However, the student gains no additional marks for this, as the question requires them to link to only one source of wisdom or authority.

The reason is developed with further information.

The answer starts well by using the words of the question and clearly stating a reason.

To support my revision, I created a set of key word revision cards. These were especially useful in helping me to learn Arabic terms used in Islam.

Improve the answer

1 A student has written the first part of their answer to this question (this paragraph looks at reasons to agree with the statement). Use the hints below to improve it.

4 "Belief in the afterlife is central to being a Muslim."

Evaluate this statement considering arguments for and against.

In your response you should:

- refer to Muslim teachings
- refer to different Muslim points of view
- reach a justified conclusion.   **(12 marks)**

Hints

- Make a clear argument in this paragraph to explain why some Muslims feel Akhirah is so important to them. Try to use evaluative language when you present each reason – for example, 'a strong argument is...' or 'another supportive valid reason is...'.
- Remember to add teachings to your answer. The student's answer refers to the Qur'an but such references need to be linked to relevant arguments and explained in more detail.

Had a go

Some Muslims may agree with the statement because they believe they need to submit to Allah in every aspect of their lives. Another reason is that Muslims believe Allah is always watching. Muslims also want to have a good afterlife, which will encourage them to hold this as an important belief. Muslims believe that paradise is a reward for being good and accepting Allah, while hell is a horrible place as described in the Qur'an. I feel there are many good reasons to support this viewpoint.

During my revision, I found it really helpful to practise the required elements of an evaluation question separately. I wasn't confident applying my knowledge to give differing viewpoints and evaluating the arguments – which are the skills required for assessing a statement – so breaking down my answers in this way helped me to focus on improving in this area.

Mark the answer

1 Draw lines to connect the marker's comments to the relevant parts of the answer. One has been done for you.

4 "Muslim beliefs about the creation of the universe are in conflict with scientific beliefs."

Evaluate this statement considering arguments for and against.

In your response you should:

- refer to Muslim teachings
- reach a justified conclusion.
- refer to different Muslim points of view

(12 marks)

> **Hints**
> Use the bulleted list in the 12-mark 'Evaluate' question as a checklist to ensure you have included all the required elements in your answer.

Nearly there

Some Muslims may strongly agree with the statement, believing that only what is written in the Qur'an is true about the creation of the universe, as the Qur'an contains the words of Allah. The Qur'an says Allah created the universe and science says it was the Big Bang; these religious and scientific accounts are very different, so they are in conflict. Another reason to agree with the statement is that science appears to suggest the universe was created by chance, while Islam teaches that Allah planned it. Although there is some good evidence for this view, I feel that it is difficult to reject science in today's modern world. Therefore, there are probably other arguments that are stronger. On the other hand, many Muslims believe science and Islam are not in conflict over the creation of the universe. They believe that science is actually part of Allah's plan in creating the universe, and that science helps them to understand better how Allah planned and made his creation. If this view is accepted, there is no conflict between Islam and science – they are in fact seen to work together. Moreover, there are some teachings in the Qur'an that Muslims point to as possibly discussing the role of science in creating the universe. This adds further evidence to the view that there is no conflict between science and religion overall.

Having considered all the arguments carefully, I have to conclude that I disagree with the statement more than I agree with it. I feel that, in today's scientific world, it is more acceptable for Muslims to look for ways of making science and Islam work together to explain the creation of the universe, rather than for these different scientific and religious accounts to be in conflict.

There is some consideration of why the point of view is valid. This approach should be applied consistently throughout the answer.

There is a successful change of argument at this point – the student goes on to explain reasons to disagree with the statement.

The answer starts with a clear focus by identifying arguments to agree with the statement.

The answer offers a justified conclusion at the end, once all the arguments have been considered.

The student has mentioned a source of authority, but no quotes or explanation are used.

Although the answer offers a conclusion, it would be stronger if the student had identified some of the more persuasive arguments and explained more clearly how they reached their conclusion.

Mark the answer

1 Use the mark scheme below to decide which level the answer on the previous page reaches.
Try to identify what you could add or change to improve the answer.

4 "Muslim beliefs about the creation of the universe are in conflict with scientific beliefs."

Evaluate this statement considering arguments for and against.

In your response you should:

- refer to Muslim teachings
- refer to different Muslim points of view
- reach a justified conclusion.

(12 marks)

Level	Descriptor
4 10–12 marks	• Clear understanding of the skill of evaluation is demonstrated with knowledge around the issues used to support judgements made. • The strengths and weaknesses of arguments are considered. • A summary conclusion is offered that justifies which is the stronger side of the argument, with supporting evidence.
3 7–9 marks	• Good understanding of the demands of the question with some, but not all, elements of the question being considered. • Arguments are used on both sides of the debate with good use of knowledge and sources of authority to support. • A reasoned conclusion is offered with some evidence, but it lacks some strength in justification.
2 4–6 marks	• Some arguments are used to address the statement, with some knowledge linked to arguments given. • A full understanding of the issues concerning the statement is lacking. • The conclusion is beginning to show some judgements but is not justified.
1 1–3 marks	• There is some attempt to address the statement and connect some basic knowledge to the question. • Knowledge is basic and limited. • The conclusion is vague and not justified.
0	• No relevant content included.

I would award the answer a Level   because

....

....

....

....

....

....

....

Mark the answer

1 Draw lines to connect the marker's comments to the relevant parts of the student's answer. One has been done for you.

1 Outline **three** reasons why Christians believe justice is important.

(3 marks)

Hints
Try to keep your answers to 3-mark 'Outline' questions brief and to the point, as they are worth the fewest marks.

Had a go

Christians believe justice is important because God is understood to be just and

Christians believe they should try to act in the same way as God. 'Treat others

as you want to be treated' is a teaching from Jesus that Christians should follow;

this shows that justice is important. A third belief is that justice makes sense

to Christians.

A valid point is given but the answer is too wordy and explains rather than outlines a Christian belief.

This final idea does not really offer a valid reason to answer the question.

This point gives an excellent teaching that links to the question but the sentence is too wordy and needs to be more direct.

2 Draw lines to connect the marker's comments to the relevant parts of the student's answer. One has been done for you.

1 Outline **three** Christian teachings about peace.

(3 marks)

Hints
Make sure you read the question carefully, as you may be asked about teachings OR beliefs. This question asks about teachings that come from a source of religious authority in Christianity such as the Bible.

Had a go

Christianity teaches 'treat others as you would want to be treated' as a message

of peace. Jesus taught 'Blessed are the peacemakers'.

Christians believe they should not hate people.

In my revision, I spent some time creating a list of teachings from the Bible that I could use to answer questions on a range of topics. It's amazing how the same teaching can be used for different topics!

This outlines a Christian belief, not a Christian teaching from a source of religious authority.

This is a clear statement about one of Jesus' teachings that successfully answers the question.

A relevant and clear Christian teaching about peace is stated.

Complete the question

1 Use the student's answer to complete the question.

1 Outline **three** .... **(3 marks)**

Nailed it!

The Church can hold coffee mornings. The Church can also organise a youth club for children to attend.

The Church may organise food banks.

I found it useful to create my own examples of questions as part of my revision. This really helped me to understand what the examiner is looking for.

2 Use the student's answer to complete the question.

1 Outline **three** .... **(3 marks)**

Nailed it!

The Trinity helps Christians to understand the nature of God. It is the idea of God as Father, Son and

Holy Spirit. It shows Christians that the three parts are equally important.

3 Use the student's answer to complete the question.

1 Outline **three** ways .... **(3 marks)**

Nailed it!

Christians send cards and give presents. They may attend Midnight Mass. They may also put on a

nativity play.

4 Use the student's answer to complete the question.

1 Outline **three** .... **(3 marks)**

Nailed it!

One condition is that there must be a reasonable chance of success. Another condition is that it must be

used only as a last resort. A third condition is that its aim must be to bring about peace.

Complete the answer

1 Complete the student's answer so that it would be awarded 3 marks.

> **1** Outline **three** reasons why Christians believe weapons of mass destruction are not acceptable. **(3 marks)**
>
> **Hints**
> - Do not waste time in the exam rewriting the question in your answer. You are simply required to identify three correct ideas.
> - Two beliefs have been given in this answer, so you need to add one more. Make sure each idea you present in your answer is different.
>
> **Nearly there**
>
> Weapons of mass destruction are considered by Christians to cause too much damage to the environment.
>
> They also kill innocent human life.
>
> ....

2 Complete the student's answer so that it would be awarded 3 marks.

> **1** Outline **three** reasons why prayer is important to Christians. **(3 marks)**
>
> **Hints**
> This time, only one reason has been given in the answer below, so you need to add two more relevant reasons.
>
> **Had a go**
>
> Prayer helps Christians to get closer to God.
>
> ....
>
> ....

3 Complete the student's answer so that it would be awarded 3 marks.

> **1** Outline **three** Christian beliefs about why the death penalty is wrong. **(3 marks)**
>
> **Had a go**
>
> Christians follow the teaching 'You shall not murder'.
>
> ....
>
> ....
>
> When I was revising for this style of question, I created flash cards with the topic on one side and three ideas about the topic on the back. They worked really well when I was testing myself or getting someone else to test me.

Mark the answer

1 Draw lines to connect the marker's comments to the relevant parts of the student's answer. One has been done for you.

2 Explain **two** ways Christians respond to help those who suffer in the world. **(4 marks)**

Had a go

Christians may choose to be involved in charity work. Many Christians have been

inspired to give money to charity or volunteer to help with the work of a charity to

ease the suffering of others. Christians may also pray.

> One response is clearly stated, with a clear and specific idea that answers the question.

> A second reason has been stated but it needs to be developed to meet the requirements of this question.

> The first reason given has been developed with further information. Adding a specific named example of a Christian charity could develop this part of the answer further.

Hints

A 4-mark 'Explain' question can be answered using four sentences in total. Aim to give each point in one sentence and then add a second sentence to explain each point made.

2 Now use the mark scheme below to decide how many marks you would award the student's answer above.

Question	Answer	Reject
2 **AO1** **4 marks**	Award one mark for providing a way and a second mark for developing the way. Up to a maximum of four marks. • Christians may respond through charity work. (1) They could donate to a charity such as Christian Aid or volunteer time when emergencies happen. (1) • Christians may respond through prayer. (1) They could pray for those who are suffering, to give them strength and remind them that people are thinking of them. (1) • Christians may respond by looking to the Bible for advice on how to understand suffering. (1) They could look to the example of Job, who suffered as a test of faith, and take comfort from the belief that God will not make people suffer more than they can bear. (1)	• Repeated reason/development • Development that does not relate both to the reason given and to the question
There may be other valid answers, but for this activity use the mark scheme given.		

I would award the answer .... marks because ....

....

....

Improve the answer

1 Write an improved answer to the question below. Use the hints to make sure your answer is awarded 4 marks.

---

2 Explain **two** ways Christians can work to reduce the causes of crime. **(4 marks)**

> **Hints**
> • You only need to explain **two** ways in which Christians can work to reduce crime.
> • Once you have identified each way, you need to develop it by adding further information. This could be more detail, an example or a Christian teaching.

Nearly there

Christian organisations such as the Street Pastors work on the streets to try to reduce the causes of crime, by providing guidance to people who may become involved in crime. Christians can also work as role models and educate young people in areas where people may live in poverty or be more likely to turn to a life of crime.

....

....

....

....

....

....

....

---

2 Write an improved answer to the question below. Use the same hints from the activity above to make sure your answer is awarded 4 marks.

---

2 Explain **two** reasons why some Christians are pacifists. **(4 marks)**

Had a go

Some Christians are pacifists because of the many Christian teachings about peace. Christians may also be pacifists because they wish to follow the example of famous Christians who have applied this view to their own actions.

....

....

....

....

....

....

....

Complete the answer

1   Complete the student's answer so that it would be awarded 4 marks.

> **2** Explain **two** reasons why Christians feel it is important to celebrate the festival of Easter.   **(4 marks)**
>
> > **Hints**
> >
> > Two ideas have been stated in the answer below, so you need to develop each one.
> > You could do this by adding a relevant example or expanding upon the reason given to show you understand it fully.

Nearly there

Easter is an important festival to Christians, as it recalls the crucifixion and celebrates the resurrection

of Jesus.

....

Easter is also an important festival because it brings the Christian community together to confirm their beliefs

about God.

....

2   Complete the student's answer so that it would be awarded 4 marks.

> **2** Explain **two** reasons why Christians believe criminals should be treated with respect.   **(4 marks)**
>
> > **Hints**
> >
> > The first reason has been stated in this answer, so you need to develop this reason by adding further information or an example. Then add a second reason and develop it in the same way.

Had a go

Christians believe that, even though criminals have done wrong, they should always be treated with respect,

and any punishment should be fair and just.

....

....

....

....

....

....

Improve the answer

1 Rewrite the student's answer to achieve the highest possible mark.

3 Explain **two** reasons why Christians believe people suffer. **(5 marks)**

In your answer you must refer to a source of wisdom and authority.

> **Hints**
> * You need to state **two** reasons and then develop each one.
> * You also need to link at least one of your reasons to a relevant source of religious authority for Christians, such as the Bible. You can do this by quoting a teaching directly or by paraphrasing a teaching (putting it in your own words).

Had a go

Christians believe one reason why people suffer is because God gave humanity free will. Another reason why

Christians believe people suffer is because suffering can be a test of faith.

....

....

....

....

....

....

....

I thought carefully about how some teachings could be applied to different topics. For example, the Bible teaching 'made in the image of God' can be used to explain the story of how God created humans to be different to all other creations, and also why Christians believe issues such as abortion and euthanasia are wrong.

Reorder the answer

1 A student has written a plan to answer the question below. Decide in which order the points should go to structure a logical answer. The one that goes first has been done for you.

---

3 Explain **two** ways the Biblical account of creation can be understood by Christians today.

In your answer you must refer to a source of wisdom and authority. **(5 marks)**

> **Hints**
>
> Think about what you might include in your response before looking at the paragraphs below to order them.

☐ They accept that God created the world, as described in the Bible, but they may argue that the biblical account is more mythical and that science helps them to understand how God was able to create the world.

☐ As all scientific theories, such as the Big Bang theory, conflict with this belief, these Christians reject science and accept only what the Bible teaches.

[1] Some literalist Christians understand the biblical account of creation to be literally true word for word, meaning that God created the world out of nothing.

☐ They look to Bible teachings such as Genesis 1:1, which says 'in the beginning God created the heavens and the Earth', and interpret this as literally true because they believe the Bible records the actual words of God.

☐ Other, non-literalist, Christians understand the story of creation as giving them important truths but not being a factual account of the creation of the universe.

> **Hints**
>
> When answering the 5-mark 'Explain' questions, remember you need to link one of your ideas to a source of religious wisdom and authority. You do not need to quote directly from the source (although you can if you wish) – you can simply state in your own words what you know it says.

Mark the answer

1 Use the mark scheme below to assign a mark to the answer. Explain your decision.

---

3 Explain **two** reasons why Christians believe forgiveness is important.

In your answer you must refer to a source of wisdom and authority. **(5 marks)**

> When answering the 5-mark 'Explain' questions, I always try to think of two ideas to include in my answer *before* I start writing. I also try to choose a religious source I can quote directly or summarise in my own words.

Nearly there

Christians believe forgiveness is important because there are many teachings from Jesus about forgiveness in the Bible, which Christians try to follow. For example, Christians look to Jesus' example when he was dying on the cross yet forgave those who put him to death: while on the cross, Jesus said, 'Father, forgive them, for they know not what they do.' Another reason why forgiveness is important is because God forgives those who sin, so Christians believe they should try to do the same.

Question	Answer
3 **AO1** **5 marks**	Award one mark for each reason and one mark for developing each reason. Up to a maximum of four marks. Award one further mark for any relevant source of wisdom and authority. • There are many teachings from Jesus that show it is important. (1) Jesus forgave those who put him to death while on the cross and Christians want to follow his example. (1) 'Father, forgive them, for they know not what they do.' (1) • God is a judge and will forgive them after death for the things they have done wrong and are sorry for. (1) Christians believe they should try to forgive others as God does, and as they expect God to forgive them. (1) Prayers such as the Lord's Prayer reinforce these beliefs through the words 'Forgive us our trespasses as we forgive those who trespass against us'. (1) • Christianity teaches that God wants humans to live in peace with each other, forgiving each other when they do wrong. (1) There are many Bible teachings that support the idea of living harmoniously with others through forgiveness. (1) Jesus taught, 'Forgive and you will be forgiven'. (1)
There may be other valid answers, but for this activity use the mark scheme given.	

I would award the answer .... marks because ....

....

....

....

Mark the answer

1 This mark scheme for Question 4 has some information missing. Complete it by putting the information below into the correct gaps. One has been done for you.

A   Sustained and accurate knowledge of religion and belief is shown for a range of viewpoints, with connections made between them.

B   The conclusion is vague and not justified.

C   The statement is addressed with logical chains of reasoning.

D   Reasoned judgements are made, leading to a partially justified conclusion.

E   Limited knowledge of religion and belief is shown.

F   Coherent and reasoned judgements are fully supported by comprehensive evidence and a fully justified conclusion is given.

G   There is some attempt to address the statement.

Hints

The more you understand what examiners are looking for, the better your answers will become.

Level	Description
4 **10–12** **marks**	• The statement is fully addressed with coherent and logical chains of thought and reasoning.
3 **7–9** **marks**	• Accurate knowledge of religion and belief is shown for different viewpoints.
2 **4–6** **marks**	• The statement is addressed with some linking of reasons. • E: Limited knowledge of religion and belief is shown. • Some weak judgements of arguments, with a conclusion that is not justified.
1 **1–3** **marks**	• Isolated knowledge of religion and belief is given.

I found it really useful to look at the level descriptors to help me understand what the examiner would be looking for in my answers. I also found it useful to sometimes work with a friend and talk through what mark we would give our answers and how we might improve them using the level descriptors for guidance.

Reorder the answer

1 A student has written a plan to answer the question below. Decide:

- which of their points support the statement
- which of their points counter the statement
- which of their points may be used in a justified conclusion.

Mark each point with an S (support), C (counter) or J (justified conclusion). One has been done for you.

---

4 "War is sometimes acceptable."

Evaluate this statement considering arguments for and against. In your response you should:

- refer to Christian teachings
- refer to different Christian points of view
- refer to relevant ethical arguments
- reach a justified conclusion.

(12 marks)

☐ Many Christians believe that Christianity teaches about peace rather than war. They look to teachings in the Bible, such as 'You shall not murder' and 'Love your enemies and pray for those who persecute you', to support this view.

☐ It is possible to argue that there is a diverse range of views within Christianity on the issue of war, ranging from those who avoid violence at all costs to those who believe there are circumstances when war may be justified.

☐ Some Christians may choose to be pacifist and believe that war and violence are never the answer. They would look to teachings from Jesus, such as 'Blessed are the peacemakers', to justify this position.

☐ Some Christians may look to ethical theories such as situation ethics, which states that each and every situation needs to be considered individually.

☐ Overall, it is up to the individual Christian to decide their stance on the statement. They may choose to look to traditional Christian teachings from the Bible and Jesus, to employ ethical theories to give guidance on what is the correct action or to use their individual conscience.

☐ There have been examples of famous Christians who have refused to use any sort of violence. The Quakers strongly believe that peaceful solutions should be sought rather than resorting to war and violence.

S Some Christians may look to the teachings of Just War theory, which has conditions that can be applied to ensure a war is justified. If the conditions are met then war is used: only as a last resort, aiming to bring peace and ensuring no innocent civilians are killed. Under these circumstances, some Christians may support war as a final option.

☐ There are some passages in the Bible that suggest war might sometimes be the right action – for example Numbers 31:1–2. There are also examples of wars being fought in the Bible, such as the Babylonian War.

I was always careful to make sure I had enough time to write my answers to these questions, as they are worth the most marks and require you to demonstrate the more difficult skills.

Mark the answer

1 Read the first part of this student's answer to the question below. Draw lines to connect the marker's comments about SPaG to the relevant parts of the answer. One has been done for you.

4 "Pilgrimage is still important for Christians today."

Evaluate this statement considering arguments for and against. In your response you should:

- refer to Christian teachings
- refer to different Christian points of view
- refer to relevant ethical arguments
- reach a justified conclusion.   **(15 marks)**

Hints

In Paper 2B, some questions have 3 extra marks available for Spelling, Punctuation and Grammar (SPaG) and your use of specialist terms. This means you should use key religious vocabulary accurately and make sure you check your answer thoroughly.

Had a go

Some Christians will agree with the statement, beliving that going on a pilgrimage means visiting places that are significant to the history of christianity. For example, visiting Bethlehem and Jerusalem (where Jesus was born and died) allows Christians to trace where the relligion started and reflect on these places. Furthermore, through visiting these places, Christians can share the experence with others, taking time out from normal life to reflect on their faith and become closer to God. Although there is no requirement in christianity to complete a pilgrimage, Christians may feel that, as many before them have completed pilgrimages, it is important for them to do this too.

Key words such as 'Christianity' (which is the name of the religion) need capital letters.

This part of the answer has good use of punctuation.

The word 'believing' is spelled incorrectly.

2 Use the mark scheme below to assign a mark for SPaG to the student's answer. There are 3 marks available for SPaG. Explain your decision.

Performance	Description
High **3 marks**	• Spelling and punctuation are used with consistent accuracy. • Rules of grammar are used with effective control of meaning. • A wide range of specialist terms is used as appropriate.
Intermediate **2 marks**	• Spelling and punctuation are used with a considerable level of accuracy. • Rules of grammar are used with general control of meaning overall. • A good range of specialist terms is used as appropriate.
Threshold **1 mark**	• Spelling and punctuation are used with a reasonable level of accuracy. • Rules of grammar are used with some control of meaning and errors do not significantly hinder meaning overall. • A limited range of specialist terms is used as appropriate.
No marks awarded	• Nothing is written or the response does not relate to the question. • Errors in spelling, punctuation and grammar make it very difficult to understand the answer.

I would give this answer _____ out of 3 marks because ....

....

Mark the answer

1 Draw lines to connect the marker's comments to each of the three different student answers below.

---

1 Outline **three** Muslim beliefs about the nature of Allah. **(3 marks)**

1 Muslims believe there is only one God because they accept the idea of Tawhid. Muslims also believe that Allah is all-powerful because he created the universe and everything within it. Muslims believe Allah is forgiving, as he will forgive those who are sorry for their mistakes after death.

Three points are given but are explained rather than stated.

2 Muslims believe Allah is the only God. They also believe he is omnipotent. A third belief is that Allah is loving and cares for his creation.

This answer starts with a sentence that is not relevant to the question being asked. It then continues by adding two valid ideas about the nature of Allah.

3 Muslims think it is important to understand what Allah is like. They believe he is the creator of the world and that he is all-powerful.

This answer successfully gives three separate valid ideas, with each one stated in its own sentence.

---

2 Use the mark scheme below to assign a mark to each student answer. Explain your decisions.

Question	Answer	Reject
1 **AO1** **3 marks**	Award one mark for each belief identified up to a maximum of three. • Muslims believe there is only one God (Tawhid). (1) • Muslims believe Allah is omnipotent (all-powerful). (1) • Muslims believe Allah is just. (1) • Muslims believe Allah is forgiving. (1) • Muslims believe Allah is omnibenevolent (all-loving). (1)	• Focus on why the characteristics of Allah are important to Muslims.
There may be other valid answers, but for this activity use the mark scheme given.		

I would award Answer 1 .... out of 3 marks because ....

....

I would award Answer 2 .... out of 3 marks because ....

....

I would award Answer 3 .... out of 3 marks because ....

....

Complete the answer

1 Complete the student's answer so that it would be awarded 3 marks.

1 Outline **three** reasons why Muslims believe humans suffer. **(3 marks)**

> **Hints**
> - Two beliefs have been given in this answer. You need to add one more.
> - Try to give each idea as a separate sentence. This will make it easier for the examiner to identify whether you have given three different reasons.

Nearly there

Muslims believe suffering is part of Allah's plan. Muslims also believe humans suffer because they abuse their free will.

....

2 Complete the student's answer so that it would be awarded 3 marks.

1 Outline **three** examples of Muslims who do not have to complete Sawm. **(3 marks)**

> **Hints**
> This time, only one reason has been given, so you need to add two more relevant reasons.

Had a go

Elderly Muslims do not have to complete Sawm.

....

....

I always make sure I read the question carefully and check what I am being asked. I've learned from past mistakes that I can get carried away and waste precious time answering the wrong question!

3 Complete the student's answer so that it would be awarded 3 marks.

1 Outline **three** Muslim teachings about peace. **(3 marks)**

Had a go

The Qur'an teaches that Allah wants Muslims to live in peace with each other as part of the ummah.

....

....

Find the answer

1 Use the marking instructions below to decide which **one** of the four points you would **not** include in your answer to the following question. Explain your choice. Then explain why you would include the other three points.

---

1 Outline **three** actions performed by Muslims on Hajj.　　　　　　　　　　　　**(3 marks)**

> **Hints**
> The skill required for 3-mark 'Outline' questions is identification of three separate ideas.

A　| Muslims wear two pieces of white cloth.

B　| Muslims circle the Ka'bah seven times.

Marking instructions
Award one mark for each point identified up to a maximum of three.

C　| Muslims believe Hajj shows commitment to Allah.

D　| Muslims stone the devil at Mina.

I would not include point　　　　because ....

....

I would include points　　　　　because ....

....

---

2 Look at this student's answer to the question below. Which **one** of the three points would be best to add to achieve the final mark?

---

1 Outline **three** Muslim beliefs about why forgiveness is important.　　　　　　　**(3 marks)**

(**Nearly there**)

> Muslims believe forgiveness is important because Allah is merciful and they should try to show forgiveness towards others in the same way. Also, Islam is seen as a religion of peace and forgiveness is part of this.

A　| Muslims believe they should forgive criminals who do wrong.

B　| Forgiving others helps you to feel better.

C　| Muslims believe they should follow the example of Muhammad, who taught that forgiveness was important.

I would include point　　　　because ....

....

....

I would **not** include point　　　　because ....

....

Reorder the answer

1 A student has written a plan to answer the question below. Decide which order the points should go in to structure a logical answer.

2 Explain **two** differences between Islamic beliefs about the afterlife and beliefs held by the main religious tradition of Great Britain.
(4 marks)

Hints

There are two topics where you could be asked to compare and contrast beliefs between Islam and the main religious tradition of Great Britain (which is Christianity). The topics are 'Beliefs about the afterlife and their significance' and 'The practice and significance of worship'. The style of question is the same – you will need to state the similarities or differences (whichever you are asked for) and then add a second sentence to develop your answer.

☐ Muslims believe angels have a role in their beliefs about the afterlife, whereas Christians do not.

☐ Muslims emphasise that the person who has done wrong has to be sorry for their sins. Christians accept this same idea but also believe that the death of Jesus atoned for the sins of the world and repaired the relationship between God and humanity.

☐ Muslims also believe that a person has to ask for forgiveness from God after death, whereas Christians believe that Jesus died for the sins of the whole world.

☐ Islam teaches that throughout a person's life, angels record a person's good and bad actions then share these with Allah after death, for him to judge whether the person should go to paradise or to hell.

When a question asked me to compare or contrast different religions, I found it useful to create a quick list of similarities and differences before I answered the question.

2 A student has written a plan to answer the question below. Decide which order the points should go in to structure a logical answer.

2 Explain **two** similarities about why worship is important in Islam and to the followers of the main religious tradition of Great Britain.
(4 marks)

☐ Muslims and Christians both believe that worship is important to develop a relationship with God.

☐ Muslims and Christians both believe that worship is important so they can ask God for help or support.

☐ Both Muslims and Christians will pray when they want to ask God for forgiveness for something they have done wrong or for help if they are struggling in their lives.

☐ They both pray regularly and have a holy day each week where they may attend a place of worship to worship with others of the same faith, so they can show commitment to God.

Improve the answer

1 Write an improved answer to the question below. Use the hints to make sure your answer is awarded 4 marks.

2 Explain **two** reasons why some Muslims do not support the use of the death penalty. **(4 marks)**

> **Hints**
> - You need to give two valid, different reasons.
> - Once you have identified each reason, develop it by adding further information. This could be an example, a teaching or a second piece of information related to the first.
> - Make sure you answer the question you have been asked! It helps to use the words of the question within your answer, to show you are focusing on it.

Had a go

Some Muslims do not support the use of the death penalty because the Qur'an teaches that it is one option but not the only option. Another reason they may not support the use of the death penalty is because they may look to teachings that show life is special.

....

....

....

....

....

....

....

2 Write an improved answer to the question below. Use the hints from the first activity to make sure your answer is awarded 4 marks.

2 Explain **two** reasons why the Six Beliefs of Islam are important to Sunni Muslims. **(4 marks)**

Had a go

The Six Beliefs of Islam are important to Sunni Muslims as they help them to understand their religion better. They will understand how Allah wants them to behave.

....

....

....

....

....

....

Complete the answer

1 Complete the student's answer so that it would be awarded 4 marks.

2 Explain **two** reasons why Muslims may sometimes support war. **(4 marks)**

> **Hints**
> One reason has been stated and developed in this answer. You need to add a second reason and develop it in the same way.

Nearly there

One reason why Muslims may sometimes support war is if it meets the conditions of Just War theory.

Muslims believe Just War theory provides rules for war that should be followed, such as war being used only

as a last resort, never targeting innocent civilians and being used as a method of bringing about peace.

....

....

....

2 Complete the student's answer so that it would be awarded 4 marks.

2 Explain **two** reasons why Salah is important for Muslims to perform. **(4 marks)**

> **Hints**
> The first reason has been stated in this answer, so you need to develop this reason by adding further information. Then add a second reason and develop it in the same way.

Had a go

Muslims believe Salah is an important duty they should perform, as it is one of the Five Pillars of Islam.

....

....

....

....

....

Mark the answer

1 Draw lines to connect the marker's comments to the relevant parts of the student's answer.
One has been done for you.

3 Explain **two** ways that jihad is understood by Muslims.

In your answer you must refer to a source of wisdom and authority.

(5 marks)

Nearly there

Jihad can be understood in many different ways by Muslims, although there are two main types. Jihad means 'striving'. One way in which jihad can be understood is through the idea of greater jihad. This is more important than the other type. The second way that jihad can be understood by Muslims is through lesser jihad. This is understood as the outer struggle to defend Islam and there is a set list of criteria that must be met to justify fighting. One of these ideas is that you should only fight in a just war, which is an idea taught in the Qur'an in Surah 2 when it says, 'Fight in the cause of Allah'.

This part of the answer is not relevant to the question; it just repeats what the question is asking.

A second way of understanding jihad has been identified successfully with good use of terminology.

Although it is good to demonstrate knowledge (in this case, what the word 'jihad' means), it is not required for this question.

The student has successfully referred to a source of religious authority – in this case, the Qur'an – which is a requirement of this style of question.

The development of the second way of understanding jihad is good, giving clear further explanation.

The first way of understanding the term 'jihad' is presented. However, the development of the idea is not relevant and there is no explanation of what Muslims understand greater jihad to be.

For this style of exam question, I found it really difficult to learn quotes word for word. But then I realised I could summarise quotes in my own words and just paraphrase what a relevant part of the Qur'an said – this is so much easier to do!

Mark the answer

1 Use the mark scheme below to decide how many marks you would award the student's answer in Activity 1 on the previous page.

> When revising for the exams, it helped me to think about how my answer would be marked.
> I used this technique a lot to improve my confidence in how to answer exam questions.

Question	Answer
3 **AO1** **5 marks**	Award one mark for each way and one mark for developing each way. Up to a maximum of four marks. Award one further mark for any relevant source of wisdom and authority. • Jihad can be understood as greater jihad. (1) This means that Muslims need to try to resist daily temptations in their lives and show commitment to Allah – for example, by praying five times a day, not drinking alcohol and studying the Qur'an. (1) The Qur'an teaches, 'establish prayer'. (1) • One way of understanding greater jihad is helping others. (1) The ummah (Muslim community) is seen as important in Islam and, through supporting others, it is understood as working for Allah. (1) Surah 9:71 teaches, 'The believing men and believing women are allies of each other'. (1) • Jihad can be understood through lesser jihad. (1) This is understood as fighting in the name of Allah. (1) The Qur'an teaches, 'Fight in the cause of Allah those who fight you'. (1)
There may be other valid answers, but for this activity use the mark scheme given.	

I would award the answer .... marks because ....

....

....

....

The improvements I would make to this answer are ....

....

Complete the answer

1 Complete the student's answer so that it would be awarded 5 marks.

3 Explain **two** reasons why Muslims believe it is important to give Zakah.

In your answer you must refer to a source of wisdom and authority. **(5 marks)**

> **Hints**
>
> In this answer, two reasons have been given and the first has been developed. You need to develop the second reason and link one of the reasons to a source of wisdom and authority.

Nearly there

Muslims believe Zakah is a duty from Allah, as it is one of the Five Pillars of Islam. They consider Zakah to be

something they have to do to please Allah so they will be rewarded with Paradise in the afterlife.

....

....

Muslims also believe Zakah is important because the money is used to help the poor and needy in society.

....

....

....

2 Complete the student's answer so that it would be awarded 5 marks.

3 Explain **two** reasons why Muslims work for peace in the world.

In your answer you must refer to a source of wisdom and authority. **(5 marks)**

> **Hints**
>
> This time, only one reason has been stated. You need to add a second reason, develop both reasons and link at least one of your reasons to a source of wisdom and authority.

Had a go

Many Muslims work for peace in the world because they believe the Qur'an contains lots of teachings about

the importance of peace.

....

....

....

....

....

....

Complete the answer

1 Complete the student's answer to achieve the highest possible mark.

4 "Completing Hajj is not relevant today."

Evaluate this statement considering arguments for and against.

In your response you should:

- refer to Muslim teachings
- reach a justified conclusion. **(15 marks)**

Hints

There are several key elements you need to include to be successful in this 15-mark 'Evaluate' question. You need to:

- include arguments both for and against the statement
- refer to Muslim teachings to support your arguments
- reach a justified conclusion in response to the statement.

There are also 3 marks available for spelling and grammar (SPaG), so make sure you check your writing carefully once you have finished your answer.

Had a go

Some Muslims would strongly disagree with the statement because completing Hajj is one of the Five Pillars of Islam. This means ....

On the other hand, some Muslims may agree with the statement, arguing that ....

In conclusion, ...

Reorder the answer

1 A student has written a plan to answer this question. Decide which of their points support the statement and which counter it. Mark each with an S (support) or C (counter). One has been done for you.

---

4 "The most important aim of punishment is for the criminal to reform."

Evaluate this statement considering arguments for and against.

In your response you should:

- refer to Muslim teachings
- refer to different Muslim points of view
- reach a justified conclusion.

(12 marks)

> **Hints**
>
> Always read the bullets in the 'Evaluate' questions carefully. Sometimes they only ask for teachings, but sometimes you have to include differing Muslim views or reference to ethical theories.
> You should also check whether there are 3 marks available for SPaG for this type of question. If there are, an instruction will be given in bold above the exam question, and the question will be worth 15 marks instead of 12.

Had a go

☐ Protecting society from dangerous criminals is seen to be important, as all human life is created by Allah and is therefore sacred. Imprisoning criminals means society is safe.

☐ Islam teaches that it is important for criminals to be given the opportunity to understand why their behaviour was wrong and to change through being sorry for what they have done. Islam teaches the importance of forgiveness, so that everyone involved can move on.

☐ While the punishment of criminals is accepted as necessary, many Muslims look to teachings that suggest people need help to change. Muslim organisations such as the Muslim Chaplains' Association or Mosaic can provide support with the rehabilitation of offenders so they understand why their actions were wrong and do not reoffend.

S Islam teaches that Allah is forgiving and gives humans a second chance, so many Muslims believe Allah wants humans to behave in a similar way towards each other. Forgiveness is part of allowing a criminal to change their behaviour.

☐ Surah 4:26–28 teaches the importance of people accepting that what they have done is wrong and trying to change their behaviour.

☐ Justice is important to Muslims, and one aim of punishment is upholding the law and making sure everyone sees that justice is achieved. Punishments may also deter others from turning to crime.

Lots of the topics studied are controversial and different Muslims have different views. Before I start writing my response, I find it useful to plan my answer by considering these different views and then identifying the reasons for each view.

Mark the answer

1 Draw lines to connect the marker's comments to the relevant parts of the student's answer.

4 "Suffering is part of Allah's plan."

Evaluate this statement considering arguments for and against. In your response you should:

- refer to Muslim teachings
- refer to different Muslim points of view
- reach a justified conclusion. **(12 marks)**

> **Hints**
> You can use the bullet points in the question as a checklist to ensure you have included all the required elements, but do not forget you need to evaluate the statement, considering arguments for and against, throughout your answer.

Nearly there

Some Muslims may agree with the statement, as Islam teaches

there is a reason and purpose to suffering given by Allah. Muslims

may accept that they cannot understand this reason, believing it is

important to have faith that Allah wouldn't make them suffer more

than they could cope with. Muslims believe that Allah is transcendent

(this is part of his nature), and this is one reason why they accept that

they may not understand Allah's purpose in creating suffering. Other

Muslims may agree that suffering is part of Allah's plan, but they may

look to the story of creation and argue that humans suffer because

Allah gave us free will.

On the other hand, some Muslims may find it difficult to believe that

suffering is part of Allah's plan, because this view goes against their

understanding of Allah's nature. Muslims believe Allah is all-loving

and cares for his creation, but this view is not compatible with Allah

allowing his creation to suffer. Some Muslims may argue that the

amount of suffering is too much, so this explanation doesn't satisfy

them. Other Muslims may believe that good can come from evil or

that suffering is a test. Again, however, these ideas are difficult to

accept. Overall, I feel that the majority of Muslims would accept that

suffering is part of Allah's plan, as they have faith in him. They would

accept that humans do not know everything and cannot understand

why Allah has allowed evil in the world.

There is a change of argument and arguments to disagree with the statement are offered. However, none of these ideas are fully explained.

The answer gives good responses to agree with the statement. It could be improved with the addition of a quote from the Qur'an.

The student has shown the diversity of Muslim views, but each point should have been taken separately and developed fully with examples.

Although there is a conclusion, it is not fully justified. Nor does it consider all the arguments that have been presented in the answer.

There is some good use of religious terminology and a link to an alternative argument about creation but it needs development.

Mark the answer

1 Use the mark scheme to decide to which of these answers you would **not** award full marks. Explain your choice.

---

1 Outline **three** events that happened in the last week of the life of Jesus. **(3 marks)**

> **Hints**
>
> For the 3-mark 'Outline' questions, you are only required to state three different ideas – you do not need to develop them.

Question	Answer	Reject
1 **AO1** **3 marks**	Award one mark for each point identified up to a maximum of three. • Jesus had the Last Supper with his disciples. (1) • Jesus was arrested in the Garden of Gethsemane. (1) • Jesus was crucified on the cross. (1) • Jesus was resurrected. (1)	• Events that did not happen in the final week. • Explanation of events.
There may be other valid answers, but for this activity use the mark scheme given.		

A One event is that Jesus shared his final meal – the Last Supper – with his disciples. Jesus was crucified on the cross. Jesus was resurrected three days after his death.

B Jesus was arrested in the garden of Gethsemane. Jesus was crucified on the cross. He was resurrected three days later.

C Jesus shared the Last Supper with his disciples. At this meal he shared bread and wine and Christians still do this today.

Answer .... would **not** get full marks because ....

....

Complete the question

1 Use the student's answer to complete the question.

> **1** Outline **three** .... **(3 marks)**
>
> One example is the resurrection of Jesus. Another is Jesus walking on water. A third example is Jesus bringing
>
> people back from the dead.
>
> I find doing lots of different activities helps keep revision interesting. For example, answering questions, improving answers, marking answers and revising my notes all helped me to feel more confident.

2 Use the student's answer to complete the question.

> **1** Outline **three** .... **(3 marks)**
>
> It helps Christians to develop a relationship with God. Jesus taught that prayer was important and showed
>
> the disciples how to pray. Also, knowing God is listening is comforting to Christians.

3 Use the student's answer to complete the question.

> **1** Outline **three** .... **(3 marks)**
>
> Christians believe in agape love. They also believe all humans were made equal by God. They also believe
>
> Jesus did not discriminate and they should follow his example.
>
> Remember, there are many possible answers for this style of question. You must make sure the three reasons you give are different to each other.

4 Use the student's answer to complete the question.

> **1** Outline **three** .... **(3 marks)**
>
> Christians can pray privately and in silence. They can also attend a Eucharist service. Some Christians may
>
> clap, sing and dance.

Complete the answer

1 Complete the student's answer so that it would be awarded 3 marks.

> **1** Outline **three** features of infant baptism. **(3 marks)**
>
> **Hints**
> Two beliefs have been given in this answer, so you are simply required to state one more. You do not need to develop the answer with further explanation or examples.

Nearly there

> Baptism happens at the font in the church. The sign of the cross is made on the baby's forehead.
>
> ....

2 Complete the student's answer so that it would be awarded 3 marks.

> **1** Outline **three** reasons why Christians believe racism is wrong. **(3 marks)**
>
> **Hints**
> This time, only one idea has been given, so you need to add two more. Make sure each idea you present in your answer is different.

Had a go

> Christians believe God created all races to be equal.
>
> ....
>
> ....

3 Complete the student's answer so that it would be awarded 3 marks.

> **1** Outline **three** ways Christians believe God is revealed. **(3 marks)**
>
> **Hints**
> This time, only one idea has been given, so you need to add two more.

Had a go

> One way is through the Bible.
>
> ....

Mark the answer

1 Draw lines to connect the marker's comments to the relevant parts of the student's answer. One has been done for you.

---

2 Explain **two** reasons why the cosmological argument is important to Christians. **(4 marks)**

> **Hints**
>
> The 4-mark 'Explain' questions can be answered using four sentences in total. Aim to give each idea in one sentence and then add a second sentence to explain each point made.

The cosmological argument is important because it reinforces Christian

understanding of the nature of God. For example, it states that God

must exist as he created the universe and that he is omnipotent and

omnibenevolent because of the powerful and loving way in which he did this.

A second reason is that it allows Christians to accept scientific theories

while also maintaining their religious beliefs. For example, the cosmological

argument suggests that God caused the Big Bang, which in turn caused the

universe to exist.

A second reason is given and clearly offers a relevant point.

The first reason given is developed with more information.

The second idea is developed with further explanation.

The first reason is stated clearly and concisely.

---

2 Now use the mark scheme below to decide how many marks you would award the answer.

Question	Answer	Reject
2 **AO1** **4 marks**	Award one mark for providing a reason. Award a second mark for development of the reason. Up to a maximum of four marks. • It demonstrates the nature of God. (1) It shows God is omnipotent, omnipresent and benevolent. (1) • It proves God must exist. (1) As the argument states that God created the universe, he must exist. (1) • It allows Christians to accept scientific theories. (1) They can accept that God caused the Big Bang, which created the universe. (1)	• Repeated reason / development. • Development that does not relate both to the reason given and to the question.
There may be other valid answers, but for this activity use the mark scheme given.		

I would award the answer _____ marks because _____

_____

Complete the answer

1 Complete the student's answer so that it would be awarded 4 marks.

2 Explain **two** reasons why Christians believe they should work for social justice. **(4 marks)**

> **Hints**
> Each of the two reasons given below will gain one mark. To gain full marks, you need to explain each reason as well. You could do this by adding another sentence to explain the idea, or by giving an example or a teaching.

Nearly there

Christians believe they should work for social justice as this is what the Bible teaches.

....

....

Christians believe they have a responsibility to work for social justice, as all humans were created the same

by God and so deserve equal treatment.

....

....

> When answering the 4-mark 'Explain' questions, I really tried to keep my answers concise and to the point.

2 Complete the student's answer so that it would be awarded 4 marks.

2 Explain **two** reasons why the local church is important. **(4 marks)**

> **Hints**
> Two developments have been given below. You need to identify the reason for each one.

....

It allows people in the local community to come together and support each other

through events such as clubs for children and support groups, where they can share their faith.

....

....

Christians can come together to worship and to celebrate events such as baptisms, weddings and festivals

such as Easter and Christmas.

Improve the answer

1 Rewrite the student's answer to achieve the highest possible mark.

2 Explain **two** reasons why miracles are important in Christianity. **(4 marks)**

Hints

Two basic reasons have been stated but the question requires them to be explained.

Had a go

Christians believe miracles are important because they are seen as evidence of a personal God acting in

the world. They are also important because they are proof of the existence of God and demonstrate his love

for his creation.

....

....

....

....

....

....

2 Rewrite the student's answer to achieve the highest possible mark.

2 Explain **two** beliefs about life after death for Christians. **(4 marks)**

Hints

Make sure the points you include in your answer are accurate and relevant. The student
answer below contains some relevant content but the ideas are not developed fully.

Had a go

Christians believe that death is not the end and that there is an afterlife. Christians also believe

in reincarnation.

....

....

....

....

....

Complete the answer

1 Complete the student's answer so that it would be awarded 5 marks.

3 Explain **two** reasons why evangelical work is important in Christianity.

In your answer you must refer to a source of wisdom and authority. **(5 marks)**

> **Hints**
>
> The 5-mark 'Explain' questions require you to:
> - give two different reasons
> - develop each reason with a full explanation
> - link at least one reason to a source of wisdom and authority, such as a teaching from the Bible.

Had a go

One reason why evangelical work is important is because spreading the religion helps to secure the future growth of the Church.

....

....

....

Another reason is that Christians feel they have a duty from God to share their faith with others, which is a teaching that comes from the Bible.

....

....

....

As part of my revision for the 5-mark 'Explain' questions, I created a set of flash cards with key Bible teachings on them. Some teachings can be used for lots of different topics. I included short Bible quotations that I could easily memorise and summarised longer teachings in my own words so they were easier for me to learn.

Mark the answer

1 Draw lines to connect the marker's comments to the relevant parts of the answer. One has been done for you.

---

3 Explain **two** reasons why Christians feel it is important for children to have a Christian upbringing.

In your answer you must refer to a source of wisdom and authority. **(5 marks)**

> **Hints**
>
> When answering 5-mark 'Explain' questions, you need to:
> * state two reasons
> * develop each reason to give a full explanation
> * link at least one of your reasons to a relevant source of religious authority for Christians, such as the Bible. You can do this by quoting a teaching directly or by paraphrasing (putting it in your own words).

Had a go

Christians feel that parents have a responsibility to introduce their children to the religion and bringing them up as Christians allows them to do this. The Church will run a Sunday school so children can learn more about Christianity and this supports parents in teaching their children about the important elements of the religion. The Bible explains the duty of raising children as Christians through teachings such as Proverbs 22:6. Another reason why Christians may feel it is important to bring children up within Christianity is because they want their family to have the support of the Christian community. Christian will parents want what is best for their children, which includes teaching them about the religion.

The student has given a second reason that is different from the first and which directly addresses the question.

The first reason is clear, concise and relevant to the question.

The first reason is supported by an example, which fully develops the reason and gives a clear explanation.

A source of wisdom and authority (the Bible) is mentioned, along with a specific reference. However, it would be better if the answer included what the teaching says rather than just stating where in the Bible it is from.

There is some development of the second reason but it is very similar to what has been said previously, so it does not really develop the point fully or adequately.

I took time to learn specific Bible teachings for each topic, so I could include them in my answers. It also helped to learn teachings that I could use across different topics.

Mark the answer

1 Use the mark scheme below to decide how many marks you would award the student's answer to this question.

3 Explain **two** reasons why Christians feel it is important for children to have a Christian upbringing.

In your answer you must refer to a source of wisdom and authority. **(5 marks)**

Had a go

Christians feel that parents have a responsibility to introduce their children to the religion and bringing them up as Christians allows them to do this. The Church will run a Sunday school so children can learn more about Christianity and this supports parents in teaching their children about the important elements of the religion. The Bible explains the duty of raising children as Christians through teachings such as Proverbs 22:6. Another reason why Christians may feel it is important to bring children up within Christianity is because they want their family to have the support of the Christian community. Christian parents want what is best for their children, which includes teaching them about the religion.

Question	Answer
3 AO1 5 marks	Award one mark for each reason and one mark for developing each reason. Up to a maximum of four marks. Award one further mark for any relevant source of wisdom and authority. • Christians believe they have a responsibility to introduce their children to Christianity. (1) Christian parents may send their children to Church-run Sunday schools so children can learn more about Christianity. (1) The Bible teaches, 'Start children off on the way they should go and even when they are old they will not turn from it' (Proverbs 22:6). (1) • Christians believe that bringing their children up as Christians will mean they have support from the Christian community. (1) The Christian community will support them by celebrating rites of passage and providing guidance for families in their local communities if they are struggling. (1) The Bible teaches in Matthew 19:13–14 that children are important to God, saying 'the kingdom of Heaven belongs to such as these'. (1) • Christians believe that God wants parents to introduce their children to Christianity by setting an example of how they should live their lives. (1) If children see their parents pray, attend church and behave as God wants them to behave, they are more likely to have faith as well. (1) The Bible teaches 'bring them up in the training and instruction of the Lord' (Ephesians 6:4). (1)
	There may be other valid answers, but for this activity use the mark scheme given.

I would award the student's answer .... marks because ....

....

....

....

....

Reorder the answer

1 A student has written a plan to answer this question. Decide which of their points support the statement and which counter it. Mark each point with an S (support) or C (counter). One has been done for you.

4 "Living in a multi-faith society is challenging for Christians."

Evaluate this statement considering arguments for and against.

In your response you should:

• refer to Christian teachings
• reach a justified conclusion. **(12 marks)**

> **Hints**
>
> Try to consider a range of arguments within your response to the 'Evaluate' questions; you need to include reasons why Christians may both agree and disagree with the statement.

Had a go

☐ Some Christians may point to examples of religious persecution, where Christians have been mistreated. They may suggest that situations where Christians have not been allowed to practise their faith show multi-faith societies are unsuccessful.

☐ Many Christians believe that in a multi-faith society there is greater tolerance and understanding of all faiths.

☐ Some Christians may focus on the benefits of living in a multi-faith society. They may point to the positive impact of food influences, musical diversity and the ability of people from differing religious backgrounds to work together.

☐ Some Christians may worry that, in a multi-faith society, the beliefs and values of some groups will be ignored because other groups outnumber them or have more influence.

☐ Some Christians may take a position of exclusivity, believing that Christianity is the one true religion and acceptance of other faiths threatens it.

☐ Many Christians look to teachings from the Bible that argue for fair and just treatment of all religious people, such as 'Treat others as you would want to be treated'. They may argue that the example of Jesus not judging others shows it is possible to live in harmony with people in a multi-faith society.

S Some Christians may find it difficult to understand the viewpoints and beliefs of other religions and this can lead to conflict and disagreement. Some religions have very different ideas to Christianity.

☐ Many Christians take a position of inclusivism, which states there is truth in all religions and it is best to accept all faiths as providing a route to God or the divine.

Mark the answer

1 Draw lines to connect the marker's comments to the relevant parts of the student's answer. One has been done for you.

---

4 "Evil and suffering mean God does not exist."

Evaluate this statement considering arguments for and against. In your response you should:

- refer to Christian teachings
- refer to different Christian points of view
- reach a justified conclusion.

(15 marks)

Nearly there

Some Christians may partly agree with this statement, as the existence of evil and suffering can be seen to challenge the nature and existence of God. Their presence contradicts the belief that God is omnibenevolent and omnipotent – Christians may question why an all-loving and all-powerful God doesn't prevent evil and suffering. This argument can lead some Christians to lose faith, as they cannot find a reasonable solution. Moreover, it is sometimes the excessive amount of suffering that causes problems: many Christians accept there is a purpose to evil in the world but question why there needs to be so much of it. While these arguments provide some valid points in response to the statement, I feel there may be stronger counter-arguments against these reasons. Christians may argue that evil and suffering have a purpose from God, although humans do not know what this is. They might also look to the example of Job in the Bible. Another reason why Christians may disagree with the statement is that there are ways to respond to evil and suffering that can bring about good. For example, many people show compassion when faced with suffering and these people may turn to charity work or prayer to support other people who suffer. The Bible teaches that Christians have a duty to help people who are suffering. A final reason to counter the statement is that many evils in the world are actually the fault of humans. The creation story in Genesis argues that humans were created by God and given free will, which means they can choose to do evil acts. I feel this side of the argument is probably stronger and that it provides convincing explanations for the existence of evil and suffering in the world.

Overall, I disagree with the statement, because I think there is a reason for evil and suffering in the world. Therefore, although these may test people's faith in God, it is possible to believe in God and still accept the presence of evil and suffering.

The answer begins by offering arguments to agree with the statement. It would be good to include some examples here.

The student changes their line of argument and begins to offer arguments to disagree with the statement.

The student makes a judgement about the strength of the points they have made so far.

There is a reference to Bible teachings, but unfortunately the answer does not explain what these teachings are.

This second reason to support the counter-arguments is good, as it gives examples of the positives that can come from evil and suffering.

The conclusion is partly justified.

The final reason given to support the counter-view is strong and links to the Bible. The student has also made a judgement about the validity of the reason.

Mark the answer

1 Use the level descriptors below to assign a mark to the student's answer on the previous page. Explain your decision.

Level	Descriptor
4 **10–12 marks**	• The statement is fully addressed, with coherent and logical chains of thought and reasoning. • Sustained and accurate knowledge of religion and belief is shown for a range of viewpoints, with connections made between them. • Coherent and reasoned judgements are fully supported by comprehensive evidence and a fully justified conclusion is given.
3 **7–9 marks**	• The statement is addressed with logical chains of reasoning. • Accurate knowledge of religion and belief is shown for different viewpoints. • Reasoned judgements are made leading to a partially justified conclusion.
2 **4–6 marks**	• The statement is addressed with some linking of reasons. • Limited knowledge of religion and belief is shown. • There are some weak judgements of arguments with a conclusion that is not justified.
1 **1–3 marks**	• There is some attempt to address the statement. • Isolated knowledge of religion and belief is given. • The conclusion is vague and not justified.

I would give this answer .... marks because ....

....

....

2 Use the mark scheme below to assign a mark for SPaG to the student's answer on the previous page. There are 3 marks available for SPaG. Explain your decision.

Performance	Descriptor
High **3 marks**	• Spelling and punctuation are used with consistent accuracy. • Rules of grammar are used with effective control of meaning. • A wide range of specialist terms is used as appropriate.
Intermediate **2 marks**	• Spelling and punctuation are used with a considerable level of accuracy. • Rules of grammar are used with general control of meaning overall. • A good range of specialist terms is used as appropriate.
Threshold **1 mark**	• Spelling and punctuation are used with a reasonable level of accuracy. • Rules of grammar are used with some control of meaning and errors do not significantly hinder meaning overall. • A limited range of specialist terms is used as appropriate.
No marks awarded	• Nothing is written or the response does not relate to the question. • Errors in spelling, punctuation and grammar make it very difficult to understand the answer.

I would give this answer .... marks because ....

....

Mark the answer

1 Draw lines to connect the marker's comments to the relevant parts of the student's answer. One has been done for you.

---

1 Outline **three** Muslim beliefs about wealth.   **(3 marks)**

> **Hints**
> You simply need to state three different beliefs to be successful in this question. You do not need to develop them with explanation or examples.

(**Had a go**)

Muslims believe that they have a duty to share what they have with others.

Muslims also believe that gambling is acceptable. A third belief is that

Muslims believe all wealth belongs to Allah and is given by Allah.

> The student has stated an accurate belief but this could be shortened so it is more direct.

> A clear belief is given about sharing wealth with others. The student could improve this point by including a key Muslim term such as Zakah.

> This statement is incorrect, as this is not a belief held by Muslims. In fact, Muslims believe wealth should be used honestly and not spent on gambling.

---

2 Draw lines to connect the marker's comments to the relevant parts of the student's answer. One has been done for you.

---

1 Outline **three** reasons why al-Qadr (predestination) is important to Muslims.   **(3 marks)**

(**Had a go**)

Muslim beliefs about al-Qadr affect how a Muslim chooses to live. One

reason why it's important is because, when Muslims live their lives aware of

this belief, they want to please Allah. Another reason why it is important is

so they will help others. Another reason it is important is because it shows

how powerful Allah is.

> This reason is stated simply and is relevant to the question.

> This sentence does not give a relevant answer to the question. It simply states that it is important, rather than giving a reason for this importance.

> This final point gives a valid reason why al-Qadr is important.

> This statement is about what a Muslim may do as a result of understanding al-Qadr, rather than giving a reason why it is important.

I found it useful to make a list of key terms used in Islam when I was revising. This helped me to understand the ideas in the exam questions, so I knew what I was being asked.

Mark the answer

1 Use the mark scheme to decide to which of these student answers you would not award full marks. Explain your choice.

1 Outline **three** activities Muslims perform on Hajj. **(3 marks)**

> **Hints**
>
> Make sure each reason you provide in your answer to the 3-mark 'Outline' question is different to the others.

Question	Answer	Reject
1 **AO1** **3 marks**	Award one mark for each point identified up to a maximum of three. • Muslims will put on ihram (white clothes). (1) • Muslims will perform Tawaf (circling of the Ka'bah). (1) • Muslims will complete sa'y (running between the hills of Safa and Marwa). (1) • Muslims will stand on Mount Arafat and pray. (1) • Muslims will throw stones at the pillars in Mina to reject evil. (1) • Muslims may celebrate Id-ul-Adha at the end of Hajj. (1)	• Reasons why Muslims perform these actions.
There may be other valid answers, but for this activity use the mark scheme given.		

A   Muslims will go to Mecca.

B   Muslims will perform Tawaf. Muslims will wear white clothes. Muslims will throw stones at the pillars in Mina.

C   Muslims will perform Tawaf, which is where they circle the Ka'bah seven times. Muslims will celebrate Id at the end of Hajj. Muslims will stand on Mount Arafat and pray to Allah.

Answer .... would **not** get full marks because ....

....

2 Use the mark scheme to explain how you might improve one of the other answers.

I would improve Answer .... by ....

....

Complete the answer

1 Complete the student's answer so that it would be awarded 3 marks.

1 Outline **three** reasons why discrimination towards people of other religions is wrong for Muslims. **(3 marks)**

> **Hints**
> Two reasons have been given in this answer. The question asks you to outline three beliefs, so you need to add one more.

Nearly there

Discrimination is wrong in Islam because Muslims are taught that Allah created all humans from all religions to
be equal. Muhammad also taught in his final sermon about the importance of treating everyone the same.

....

....

2 Complete the student's answer so that it would be awarded 3 marks.

1 Outline **three** reasons why Muslims believe it is important to stand up for human rights. **(3 marks)**

> **Hints**
> This time, only one reason has been given, so you need to add two more relevant reasons. Try to make your answers clear and direct, making sure each reason is different from the other two.

Had a go

Muslims believe that all humans were created by Allah so human life is special.

....

....

....

> The 3-mark 'Outline' questions are worth the least marks, so I always made sure I didn't waste time by adding more information to develop my ideas. I simply stated three reasons, then moved on to the longer questions that are worth more marks.

Mark the answer

1   Draw lines to connect the marker's comments to the relevant parts of the student's answer.
    One has been done for you.

2   Describe **two** differences between Muslim forms of worship and the forms of worship of the main religious
    tradition of Great Britain.   **(4 marks)**

> **Hints**
>
> The 4-mark 'Describe' questions require you to compare similarities or differences between
> Islam and the main religious tradition of Great Britain, which is Christianity. They will only
> appear in questions relating to beliefs about the afterlife and the significance of worship
> practices, so make sure you have practised this type of question for these topics.

Nearly there

When Muslims pray, they do not sit down but instead move in a series of

prayer movements called rak'ahs whereas, in Christianity, Christians usually

kneel or sit when they pray.

When Muslims pray in the mosque, men and women are in different

rooms so they are fully focused on Allah and not distracted. In contrast,

men and women in Christianity usually pray together, standing side by

side and not in different rooms.

> In the second part of this answer, the student
> correctly identifies that Muslim men and
> women pray in different rooms. The reason for
> this is stated but it is not needed to answer
> the question.

> The development of this first
> idea identifies how Christianity
> (the main religious tradition in
> Britain) differs from Islam in
> terms of the way Christians pray.

> The development of this idea
> successfully identifies what is
> different in Christianity – in this
> case, that men and women
> pray together.

> The student answer shows
> knowledge of worship in Islam
> and states the method Muslims
> use when praying.

Mark the answer

1 Draw lines to connect the marker's comments to the relevant parts of the student's answer. One has been done for you.

---

2 Explain **two** actions performed by Muslims to reduce inequality in the world. **(4 marks)**

Nearly there

Muslims can take part in charity work with groups such as Islamic Relief or Muslim Aid. Muslims can also help to educate people about inequality and gather support to improve the lives of others. With charity work, Muslims could volunteer or donate money, which can be used to help in emergency situations such as when people have been left homeless after a natural disaster. When educating people about inequality, Muslims could share the message that Allah created all humans equally and that we all have a duty to help others.

> A second action is given that is different to the first.

> This development gives specific examples. However, it would be better to put this information before the second reason is introduced.

> The first action has been stated clearly and concisely, giving an accurate and relevant response to the question.

> The answer ends with development of the second action, but this should be stated directly after the reason is given.

---

2 Now use the mark scheme below to decide how many marks you would award the student's answer above. Explain your decision.

Question	Answer	Reject
2 **AO1** **4 marks**	Award one mark for each action and a second idea for developing each action. Up to a maximum of four marks. • Muslims may take part in charity work such as with Muslim Aid or Islamic Relief. (1) They could provide emergency relief after disasters. (1) • Muslims may help to educate people about issues surrounding inequality. (1) Muslims could share the message that Allah created all humans equally so everyone can work to help those facing inequality in the world. (1) • Muslims can give Zakah. (1) It is considered a duty from Allah to help others by giving money to charity, to help reduce inequality in the world. (1)	• Repeated reason/development. • Development that does not relate both to the reason given and to the question.
There may be other valid answers, but for this activity use the mark scheme given.		

I would award the answer .... marks because ....

....

....

....

Complete the answer

1 Complete the student's answer so that it would be awarded 4 marks.

2 Explain **two** reasons why miracles are important in Islam.   **(4 marks)**

> **Hints**
>
> Each of the reasons given below will gain one mark. To gain full marks, you need to explain each reason as well. You could do this by adding another sentence to explain the idea or by giving an example or a teaching.

Nearly there

Miracles are important because they help to confirm Muslim beliefs about Allah.

....

....

It is stated in the Qur'an that miracles happen so they are important in confirming what the Islamic source of

authority states.

....

....

....

> I made sure I was really clear about the different styles of question that would come up before I went into the exam. This helped me to feel confident about my ability to respond well to the questions and achieve high marks.

2 Complete the student's answer so that it would be awarded 4 marks.

2 Explain **two** activities performed to celebrate Id-ul-Fitr.   **(4 marks)**

> **Hints**
>
> One activity has been identified; you need to develop this idea by adding further explanation and then think of a second activity and develop it in the same way.

Had a go

One activity that takes place to celebrate Id-ul-Fitr is that special mosque services are held.

....

....

....

....

Improve the answer

1 Rewrite the student's answer to achieve the highest possible mark. Use the hints to help you.

3 Explain **two** reasons why the existence of suffering poses a challenge for Muslims.

In your answer you must refer to a source of wisdom and authority. **(5 marks)**

Had a go

Suffering poses a challenge for Muslims, as they believe Allah is all-loving and question why, if this is the

case, he allows his creation to suffer. 'In the name of Allah, the most loving.'

Suffering is also a challenge for Muslims as it allows some people to question whether Allah is all-powerful.

Hints

- This answer shows good knowledge of the problem of suffering, but the reasons given need to be developed and not just stated.
- A reference is made to a source of authority for Muslims, but it is not quoted accurately or explained fully and it is not linked to the question.
- The question asks why suffering is a challenge for Muslims but parts of the answer refer to how Muslims should cope with suffering. These are not relevant.
- It is best to use religious terminology within an answer wherever possible – for example, 'all-loving' could be changed to 'beneficent' or 'omnibenevolent'.

....

....

....

....

....

....

....

....

....

....

There were times during my revision where I got halfway through a practice answer and didn't know what to write next because I hadn't planned it. This taught me the importance of planning my answer before I started writing – and thankfully I didn't make that mistake in the exam!

Reorder the answer

1. A student has written a plan to answer the question below. Decide which order the points should go in to structure a logical answer. One has been done for you.

---

3. Explain **two** Muslim beliefs about the importance of social justice.

In your answer you must refer to a source of wisdom and authority.

(5 marks)

> **Hints**
>
> Remember that a logical order for answering this style of question is to state the first idea and develop it fully (linking to a source of wisdom and authority if possible) before moving on to state and develop the second idea (linking to a source of wisdom and authority if one hasn't already been included).

☐ Surah 7 says that those who have honoured Allah and followed the way he wants them to live will be successful.

☐ A second reason why Muslims believe social justice is important is that Muslims believe they will be judged by Allah after death, based on the way they have cared for his creation and looked after People in the world.

☐ Muslims believe that all humans were made by Allah, a belief stated in the Qur'an. Therefore, Muslims are expected to work to ensure there is fairness between humans and that everyone has enough to survive.

☐ Muslims take this quote to mean that Allah is always watching and wants them to support each other and bring fairness to the world. They believe he will reward those who help others with paradise in the afterlife.

[1] Muslims believe social justice is important, as they have a duty from Allah to work for social justice and bring fairness to the world. This is a key belief in Islam that can be seen through actions such as Zakah (charity).

> When answering the 5-mark 'Explain' questions, I always tried to think of two ideas to include in my answer before I started writing. I also tried to choose a religious source I could quote directly or summarise in my own words to support at least one of my reasons.

Mark the answer

1 Use the mark scheme below to assign a mark to the student's answer. Explain your decision.

3 Explain **two** reasons why angels are understood to have importance in Islam.

In your answer you must refer to a source of wisdom and authority. **(5 marks)**

> **Hints**
>
> Try to think about the structure of your answer when answering this style of question: state and develop your first reason, before giving a second reason. Remember that you also need to link one reason to a relevant and appropriate source of authority.

Had a go

Angels are important in Islam for many reasons. One of these is because they are seen to be the connection between Allah and humanity and they have brought many important messages, such as Jibril's message.

Another reason is because angels are seen to have important roles in Islam. This can be seen through Izra'il. The Qur'an states that the angel of death will take humans after death, showing that angels have roles they need to perform.

Question	Answer
3 AO1 5 marks	Award one mark for each reason and one mark for developing each reason. Up to a maximum of four marks. Award one further mark for any relevant source of wisdom and authority. • Angels have brought messages to humanity. (1) This can be seen through Jibril bringing the Qur'an to Muhammad. (1) 'And the one who has brought the truth' (Surah 39:33). (1) • Angels are mentioned many times in the Qur'an, showing their importance. (1) Specific angels that are mentioned include Jibril, Mika'il and Izra'il. (1) Surah 2 mentions these angels and talks of anyone not following their guidance as not following the faith of Islam. (1) • Angels are given specific roles in Islam, showing their importance. (1) For example, Izra'il is the angel of death. (1) 'The angel of death will take you who has been entrusted with you' (Surah 32:11). (1)
There may be other valid answers, but for this activity use the mark scheme given.	

I would award the answer .... marks because ....

....

....

> I found looking at good and bad answers really helped me to understand what the examiner was looking for, which in turn helped me to improve the quality of my answers.

Improve the answer

1 Write an improved answer to the question below. Use the hints to make sure your answer achieves the highest possible mark.

4 "Religious experience is the best way for Muslims to experience Allah."

Evaluate this statement considering arguments for and against. In your response you should:

- refer to Muslim teachings
- refer to different Muslim points of view

- reach a justified conclusion.

(15 marks)

Had a go

Some Muslims may agree with the statement as religious experience is a direct way of experiencing Allah and is a unique experience. Sufi Muslims especially may believe this. Also, religious experience demonstrates many characteristics of Allah, such as omnipotence and his omnibenevolence in wanting to act within the world. However, other Muslims may place less emphasis on religious experience. Although they accept the relevance of experiences such as the one Muhammad had when he received the Qur'an, they may believe it is more important to experience Allah through other sources. In conclusion, I feel there are good arguments on both sides of this debate.

Hints

This answer includes the main parts required by the question. However, none of these elements is fully expanded, so each element needs to be developed.

....

....

....

....

....

....

....

....

....

....

....

....

....

....

....

....

Reorder the answer

1 A student has written a plan to answer this question. Decide which of their points support the statement, which counter it and which may be used in a justified conclusion. Mark each point with an S (support), C (counter) or J (justified conclusion). One has been done for you.

4 "We all have a duty to work for racial harmony in the world."

Evaluate this statement considering arguments for and against.

In your response you should:

- refer to Muslim teachings
- reach a justified conclusion.

(12 marks)

> **Hints**
>
> Always read the bullets in the statement questions carefully. Sometimes they only ask for teachings, but sometimes you have to include differing Muslim views or reference to ethical theories. You should also check whether there are 3 marks available for SPaG for this type of question. If there are, an instruction will be given in bold above the exam question, and the question will be worth 15 marks instead of 12.

☐ Muslims believe Allah created all humans equally and they should all have equal treatment, regardless of race. There are many teachings in the Qur'an that support this view, stating that all humans are descended from Adam and Eve and deserve equal respect and treatment.

☐ There is more evidence to agree with the statement than to disagree with it, suggesting the right thing to do is to support others who may be facing racial persecution.

☐ There have been situations where people have stood up for racial equality and lost their lives or faced persecution as a result. Although racial harmony and helping others are important, you also need to respect your own life and contribute only when it is safe to do so.

☐ There are many examples of Muslims who have campaigned for racial equality. Muhammad Ali and Malcolm X both did this, although they used different methods to try and achieve their aims.

☐ If everyone followed ideas such as treating people the same, it would reduce the amount of racial incidents and bring equality to the world.

☐ There are many Muslim organisations that campaign non-violently against racism. Muslim ARC is one example.

☒ S Muhammad declared in his final sermon that 'there is no difference between Arabs and non-Arabs', meaning racism is wrong and people from all races are equal.

☐ Sometimes, individual people cannot do much to overcome differences. It may be up to governments or those with authority to bring about changes in the law to ensure there is racial harmony.

Complete the answer

1 Complete the student's answer to achieve the highest possible mark.

4 "Beliefs about life after death should be the main focus of living life."

Evaluate this statement considering arguments for and against.

In your response you should:

- refer to Muslim teachings
- refer to different Muslim points of view
- reach a justified conclusion. **(15 marks)**

> **Hints**
> - There will be various arguments in response to statement questions, so you need to consider reasons why Muslims may agree or disagree with the issue.
> - There are 3 extra SPaG marks available for this question, so check your writing carefully once you have finished your answer.

Some Muslims would agree that beliefs about life after death should direct their behaviour in life. This is because

....

....

....

They may also agree with the statement because

....

....

....

....

On the other hand, some Muslims may look at this statement differently and believe that, while life after

death is important, so too is life itself. Muslims believe

....

....

....

In conclusion, I feel that the stronger side of the argument is

....

....

....

....

....

Answers

Mark the answer

1 Draw lines to connect the marker's comments to the relevant parts of the student's answer. One has been done for you.

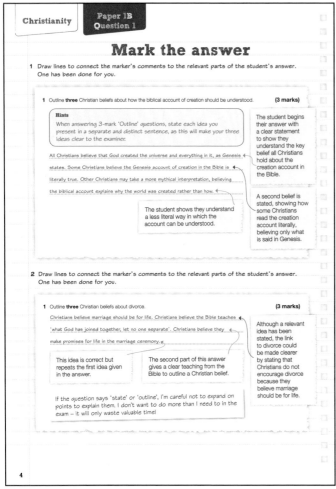

1 Outline **three** Christian beliefs about how the biblical account of creation should be understood. **(3 marks)**

Hints
When answering 3-mark 'Outline' questions, state each idea you present in a separate and distinct sentence, as this will make your three ideas clear to the examiner.

All Christians believe that God created the universe and everything in it, as Genesis states. Some Christians believe the Genesis account of creation in the Bible is literally true. Other Christians may take a more mythical interpretation, believing the biblical account explains why the world was created rather than how.

The student begins their answer with a clear statement to show they understand the key belief all Christians hold about the creation account in the Bible.

A second belief is stated, showing how some Christians read the creation account literally, believing only what is said in Genesis.

The student shows they understand a less literal way in which the account can be understood.

2 Draw lines to connect the marker's comments to the relevant parts of the student's answer. One has been done for you.

1 Outline **three** Christian beliefs about divorce. **(3 marks)**

Christians believe marriage should be for life. Christians believe the Bible teaches 'what God has joined together, let no one separate'. Christians believe they make promises for life in the marriage ceremony.

This idea is correct but repeats the first idea given in the answer.

The second part of this answer gives a clear teaching from the Bible to outline a Christian belief.

Although a relevant idea has been stated, the link to divorce could be made clearer by stating that Christians do not encourage divorce because they believe marriage should be for life.

If the question says 'state' or 'outline', I'm careful not to expand on points to explain them. I don't want to do more than I need to in the exam – it will only waste valuable time!

4

Mark the answer

1 Use the mark scheme to decide to which of the answers below you would **not** award full marks. Explain your choice.

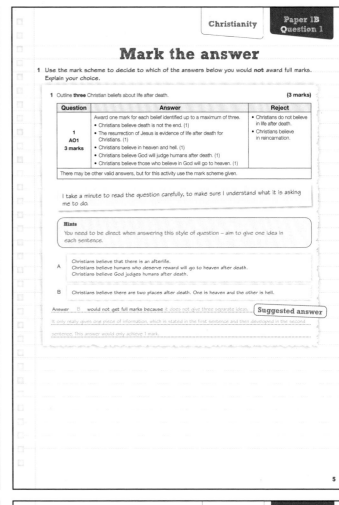

1 Outline **three** Christian beliefs about life after death. **(3 marks)**

Question	Answer	Reject
1 AO1 3 marks	Award one mark for each belief identified up to a maximum of three. • Christians believe death is not the end. (1) • The resurrection of Jesus is evidence of life after death for Christians. (1) • Christians believe in heaven and hell. (1) • Christians believe God will judge humans after death. (1) • Christians believe those who believe in God will go to heaven. (1)	• Christians do not believe in life after death. • Christians believe in reincarnation.

There may be other valid answers, but for this activity use the mark scheme given.

I take a minute to read the question carefully, to make sure I understand what it is asking me to do.

Hints
You need to be direct when answering this style of question – aim to give one idea in each sentence.

A   Christians believe that there is an afterlife. Christians believe humans who deserve reward will go to heaven after death. Christians believe God judges humans after death.

B   Christians believe there are two places after death. One is heaven and the other is hell.

Answer   B   would not get full marks because it does not give three separate ideas. [Suggested answer]

It only really gives one piece of information, which is stated in the first sentence and then developed in the second sentence. This answer would only achieve 1 mark.

5

Complete the answer

1 Complete the student's answer so that it would be awarded 3 marks.

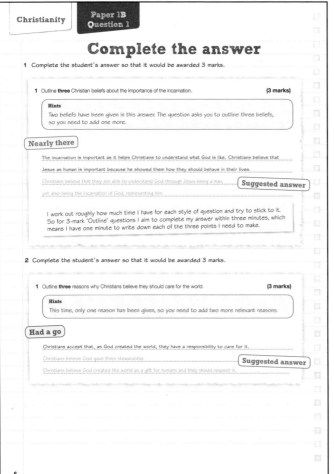

1 Outline **three** Christian beliefs about the importance of the incarnation. **(3 marks)**

Hints
Two beliefs have been given in this answer. The question asks you to outline three beliefs, so you need to add one more.

Nearly there

The incarnation is important as it helps Christians to understand what God is like. Christians believe that Jesus as human is important because he showed them how they should behave in their lives. Christians believe that they are able to understand God through Jesus being a man, yet also being the incarnation of God, representing him. [Suggested answer]

I work out roughly how much time I have for each style of question and try to stick to it. So for 3-mark 'Outline' questions I aim to complete my answer within three minutes, which means I have one minute to write down each of the three points I need to make.

2 Complete the student's answer so that it would be awarded 3 marks.

1 Outline **three** reasons why Christians believe they should care for the world. **(3 marks)**

Hints
This time, only one reason has been given, so you need to add two more relevant reasons.

Had a go

Christians accept that, as God created the world, they have a responsibility to care for it. Christians believe God gave them stewardship. Christians believe God created the world as a gift for humans and they should respect it. [Suggested answer]

6

Complete the answer

1 Complete the student's answer so that it would be awarded 4 marks.

2 Explain **two** reasons why the biblical account of creation is important for Christians today. **(4 marks)**

Hints
Each of the two reasons given below will gain 1 mark. To gain full marks, each reason needs development. This could be done by adding another sentence of information, an example or a religious teaching.

Nearly there

The story of creation in the Bible is important to Christians today because it confirms their belief that God created the universe and everything in it. It shows the nature of God – for example, being powerful enough to be able to create such an amazing universe. [Suggested answer]

Nearly there

It is important because it helps Christians to understand why the world was created. Many Christians today believe science helps to explain how God created the world, but the Genesis account explains why it was made – as a gift for humans. [Suggested answer]

2 Complete the student's answer so that it would be awarded 4 marks.

2 Explain **two** reasons why the existence of evil and suffering in the world challenges the nature of God. **(4 marks)**

Hints
Make sure that the explanation you give is specific to the nature (characteristics) of God.

Nearly there

Evil and suffering in the world may challenge the Christian belief in God as omnipotent. Christians may question why an all-powerful God doesn't prevent evil and suffering or use his power to reduce the amount of suffering. [Suggested answer]

Evil and suffering may also challenge the Christian belief in God as benevolent. Christians may question whether God actually loves his creation or cares for humanity if he allows so many people to suffer so horrifically. [Suggested answer]

I created flash cards to help me learn key words when revising, so I could use them accurately in my answers.

7

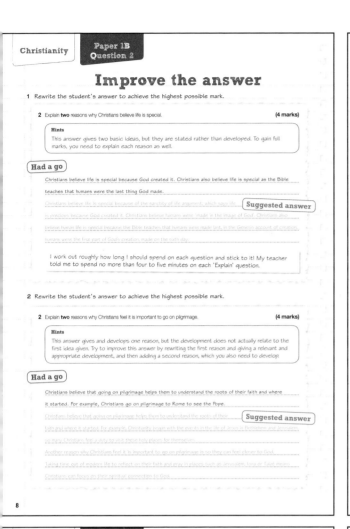

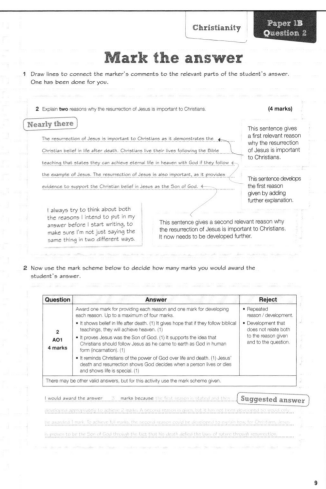

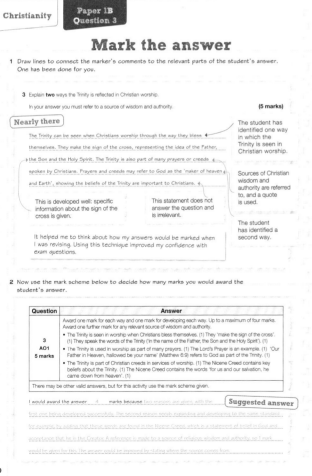

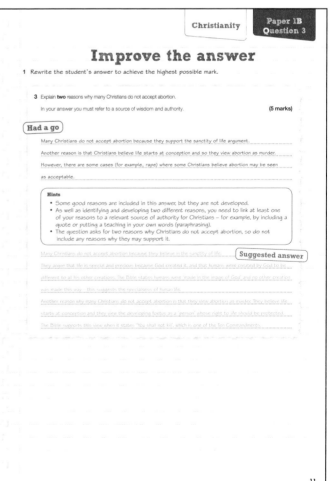

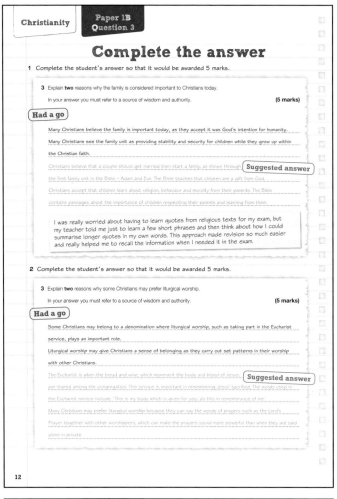

Christianity — Paper 1B Question 3

Complete the answer

1 Complete the student's answer so that it would be awarded 5 marks.

3 Explain **two** reasons why the family is considered important to Christians today.

In your answer you must refer to a source of wisdom and authority.

(5 marks)

Had a go

Many Christians believe the family is important today, as they accept it was God's intention for humanity.

Many Christians see the family unit as providing stability and security for children while they grow up within the Christian faith.

Christians believe that a couple should get married then start a family, as shown through the first family unit in the Bible – Adam and Eve. The Bible teaches that children are a gift from God. Christians accept that children learn about religion, behaviour and morality from their parents. The Bible contains passages about the importance of children respecting their parents and learning from them.

Suggested answer

I was really worried about having to learn quotes from religious texts for my exam, but my teacher told me just to learn a few short phrases and then think about how I could summarise longer quotes in my own words. This approach made revision so much easier and really helped me to recall the information when I needed it in the exam.

2 Complete the student's answer so that it would be awarded 5 marks.

3 Explain **two** reasons why some Christians may prefer liturgical worship.

In your answer you must refer to a source of wisdom and authority.

(5 marks)

Had a go

Some Christians may belong to a denomination where liturgical worship, such as taking part in the Eucharist service, plays an important role.

Liturgical worship may give Christians a sense of belonging as they carry out set patterns in their worship with other Christians.

The Eucharist is when the bread and wine, which represent the body and blood of Jesus, are shared among the congregation. This service is important in remembering Jesus' sacrifice. The words used in the Eucharist service include, 'This is my body which is given for you; do this in remembrance of me.'

Many Christians may prefer liturgical worship because they can say the words of prayers such as the Lord's Prayer together with other worshippers, which can make the prayers sound more powerful than when they are said alone in private.

Suggested answer

12

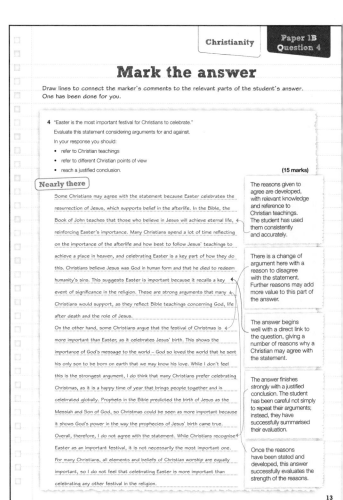

Christianity — Paper 1B Question 4

Mark the answer

Draw lines to connect the marker's comments to the relevant parts of the student's answer. One has been done for you.

4 "Easter is the most important festival for Christians to celebrate."

Evaluate this statement considering arguments for and against.

In your response you should:
• refer to Christian teachings
• refer to different Christian points of view
• reach a justified conclusion.

(15 marks)

Nearly there

Some Christians may agree with the statement because Easter celebrates the resurrection of Jesus, which supports belief in the afterlife. In the Bible, the Book of John teaches that those who believe in Jesus will achieve eternal life, reinforcing Easter's importance. Many Christians spend a lot of time reflecting on the importance of the afterlife and how best to follow Jesus' teachings to achieve a place in heaven, and celebrating Easter is a key part of how they do this. Christians believe Jesus was God in human form and that he died to redeem humanity's sins. This suggests Easter is important because it recalls a key event of significance in the religion. These are strong arguments that many Christians would support, as they reflect Bible teachings concerning God, life after death and the role of Jesus.

On the other hand, some Christians argue that the festival of Christmas is more important than Easter, as it celebrates Jesus' birth. This shows the importance of God's message to the world – God so loved the world that he sent his only son to be born on earth that we may know his love. While I don't feel this is the strongest argument, I do think that many Christians prefer celebrating Christmas, as it is a happy time of year that brings people together and is celebrated globally. Prophets in the Bible predicted the birth of Jesus as the Messiah and Son of God, so Christmas could be seen as more important because it shows God's power in the way the prophecies of Jesus' birth came true. Overall, therefore, I do not agree with the statement. While Christians recognise Easter as an important festival, it is not necessarily the most important one. For many Christians, all elements and beliefs of Christian worship are equally important, so I do not feel that celebrating Easter is more important than celebrating any other festival in the religion.

The reasons given to agree are developed, with relevant knowledge and reference to Christian teachings. The student has used them consistently and accurately.

There is a change of argument here with a reason to disagree with the statement. Further reasons may add more value to this part of the answer.

The answer begins well with a direct link to the question, giving a number of reasons why a Christian may agree with the statement.

The answer finishes strongly with a justified conclusion. The student has been careful not simply to repeat their arguments; instead, they have successfully summarised their evaluation.

Once the reasons have been stated and developed, this answer successfully evaluates the strength of the reasons.

13

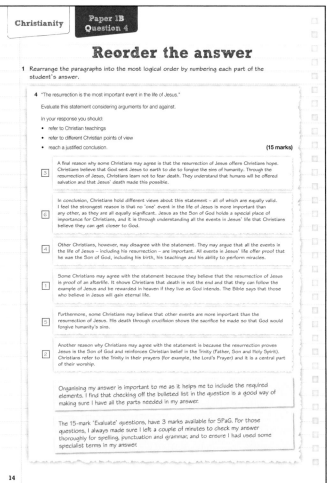

Christianity — Paper 1B Question 4

Reorder the answer

1 Rearrange the paragraphs into the most logical order by numbering each part of the student's answer.

4 "The resurrection is the most important event in the life of Jesus."

Evaluate this statement considering arguments for and against.

In your response you should:
• refer to Christian teachings
• refer to different Christian points of view
• reach a justified conclusion.

(15 marks)

[3] A final reason why some Christians may agree is that the resurrection of Jesus offers Christians hope. Christians believe that God sent Jesus to earth to die to forgive the sins of humanity. Through the resurrection of Jesus, Christians learn not to fear death. They understand that humans will be offered salvation and that Jesus' death made this possible.

[6] In conclusion, Christians hold different views about this statement – all of which are equally valid. I feel the strongest reason is that no 'one' event in the life of Jesus is more important than any other, as they are all equally significant. Jesus as the Son of God holds a special place of importance for Christians, and it is through understanding all the events in Jesus' life that Christians believe they can get closer to God.

[4] Other Christians, however, may disagree with the statement. They may argue that all the events in the life of Jesus – including his resurrection – are important. All events in Jesus' life offer proof that he was the Son of God, including his birth, his teachings and his ability to perform miracles.

[1] Some Christians may agree with the statement because they believe that the resurrection of Jesus is proof of an afterlife. It shows Christians that death is not the end and that they can follow the example of Jesus and be rewarded in heaven if they live as God intends. The Bible says that those who believe in Jesus will gain eternal life.

[5] Furthermore, some Christians may believe that other events are more important than the resurrection of Jesus. His death through crucifixion shows the sacrifice he made so that God would forgive humanity's sins.

[2] Another reason why Christians may agree with the statement is because the resurrection proves Jesus is the Son of God and reinforces Christian belief in the Trinity (Father, Son and Holy Spirit). Christians refer to the Trinity in their prayers (for example, the Lord's Prayer) and it is a central part of their worship.

Organising my answer is important to me as it helps me to include the required elements. I find that checking off the bulleted list in the question is a good way of making sure I have all the parts needed in my answer.

The 15-mark 'Evaluate' questions, have 3 marks available for SPaG. For those questions, I always made sure I left a couple of minutes to check my answer thoroughly for spelling, punctuation and grammar, and to ensure I had used some specialist terms in my answer.

14

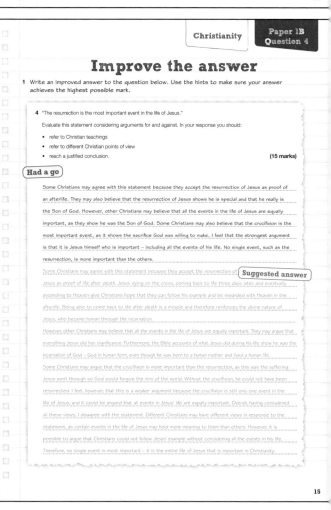

Christianity — Paper 1B Question 4

Improve the answer

1 Write an improved answer to the question below. Use the hints to make sure your answer achieves the highest possible mark.

4 "The resurrection is the most important event in the life of Jesus."

Evaluate this statement considering arguments for and against. In your response you should:
• refer to Christian teachings
• refer to different Christian points of view
• reach a justified conclusion.

(15 marks)

Had a go

Some Christians may agree with this statement because they accept the resurrection of Jesus as proof of an afterlife. They may also believe that the resurrection of Jesus shows he is special and that he really is the Son of God. However, other Christians may believe that all the events in the life of Jesus are equally important, as they show he was the Son of God. Some Christians may also believe that the crucifixion is the most important event, as it shows the sacrifice God was willing to make. I feel that the strongest argument is that it is Jesus himself who is important – including all the events of his life. No single event, such as the resurrection, is more important than the others.

Some Christians may agree with this statement because they accept the resurrection of

Suggested answer

Jesus as proof of life after death. Jesus dying on the cross, coming back to life three days later, and eventually ascending to Heaven give Christians hope that they can follow his example and be rewarded with Heaven in the afterlife. Being able to come back to life after death is a miracle and therefore reinforces the divine nature of Jesus, who became human through the incarnation.

However, other Christians may believe that all the events in the life of Jesus are equally important. They may argue that everything Jesus did has significance. Furthermore, the Bible accounts of what Jesus did during his life show he was the incarnation of God – God in human form, even though he was born to a human mother and lived a human life.

Some Christians may argue that the crucifixion is more important than the resurrection, as this was the suffering Jesus went through so God would forgive the sins of the world. Without the crucifixion, he could not have been resurrected. I feel, however, that this is a weaker argument because the crucifixion is still only one event in the life of Jesus, and it could be argued that all events in Jesus' life are equally important. Overall, having considered all these views, I disagree with the statement. Different Christians may have different views in response to the statement, as certain events in the life of Jesus may hold more meaning to them than others. However, it is possible to argue that Christians could not follow Jesus' example without considering all the events in his life. Therefore, no single event is most important – it is the entire life of Jesus that is important in Christianity.

15

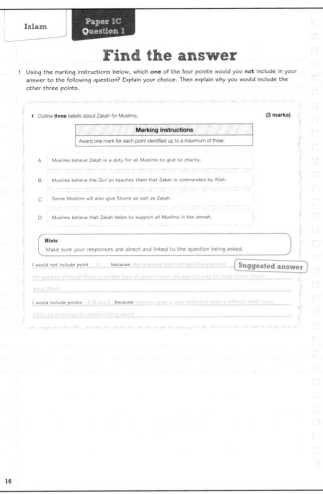

Islam — Paper 1C Question 1

Find the answer

1 Using the marking instructions below, which **one** of the four points would you **not** include in your answer to the following question? Explain your choice. Then explain why you would include the other three points.

1 Outline **three** beliefs about Zakah for Muslims. (3 marks)

Marking instructions
Award one mark for each point identified up to a maximum of three.

A Muslims believe Zakah is a duty for all Muslims to give to charity.

B Muslims believe the Qur'an teaches them that Zakah is commanded by Allah.

C Some Muslims will also give Khums as well as Zakah.

D Muslims believe that Zakah helps to support all Muslims in the ummah.

Hints
Make sure your responses are direct and linked to the question being asked.

I would not include point _____ C _____ **because** this response does not specifically answer **Suggested answer**
the question. Although Khums is another type of giving in Islam, the question asks for three Muslim beliefs
about Zakah.

I would include points _____ A, B and D _____ **because** each one gives a clear statement about a different belief about
Zakah, so answering the question being asked.

16

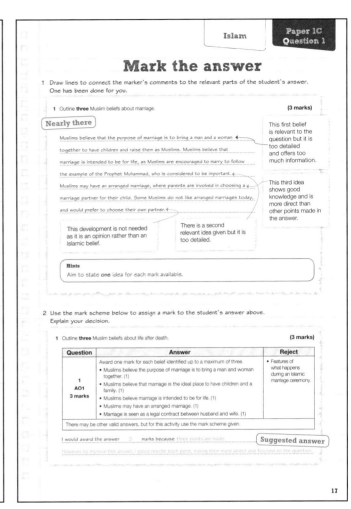

Islam — Paper 1C Question 1

Mark the answer

1 Draw lines to connect the marker's comments to the relevant parts of the student's answer. One has been done for you.

1 Outline **three** Muslim beliefs about marriage. (3 marks)

Nearly there

Muslims believe that the purpose of marriage is to bring a man and a woman together to have children and raise them as Muslims. Muslims believe that marriage is intended to be for life, as Muslims are encouraged to marry to follow the example of the Prophet Muhammad, who is considered to be important. Muslims may have an arranged marriage, where parents are involved in choosing a marriage partner for their child. Some Muslims do not like arranged marriages today, and would prefer to choose their own partner.

This first belief is relevant to the question but it is too detailed and offers too much information.

This third idea shows good knowledge and is more direct than other points made in the answer.

This development is not needed as it is an opinion rather than an Islamic belief.

There is a second relevant idea given but it is too detailed.

Hints
Aim to state **one** idea for each mark available.

2 Use the mark scheme below to assign a mark to the student's answer above. Explain your decision.

1 Outline **three** Muslim beliefs about life after death. (3 marks)

Question	Answer	Reject
1 AO1 3 marks	Award one mark for each belief identified up to a maximum of three. • Muslims believe the purpose of marriage is to bring a man and woman together. (1) • Muslims believe that marriage is the ideal place to have children and a family. (1) • Muslims believe marriage is intended to be for life. (1) • Muslims may have an arranged marriage. (1) • Marriage is seen as a legal contract between husband and wife. (1)	• Features of what happens during an Islamic marriage ceremony.
	There may be other valid answers, but for this activity use the mark scheme given.	

I would award the answer _____ 3 _____ marks **because** three points are made. **Suggested answer**
However, to improve this answer, I would rewrite each point, making them more direct and focused on the question.

17

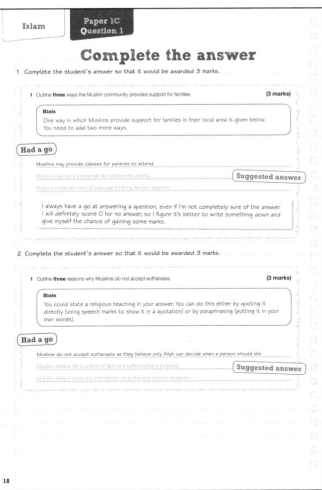

Islam — Paper 1C Question 1

Complete the answer

1 Complete the student's answer so that it would be awarded 3 marks.

1 Outline **three** ways the Muslim community provides support for families. (3 marks)

Hints
One way in which Muslims provide support for families in their local area is given below. You need to add two more ways.

Had a go

Muslims may provide classes for parents to attend.

Muslims may run a madrassah for children to attend. **Suggested answer**

Muslims celebrate rites of passage to bring families together.

I always have a go at answering a question, even if I'm not completely sure of the answer. I will definitely score 0 for no answer, so I figure it's better to write something down and give myself the chance of gaining some marks.

2 Complete the student's answer so that it would be awarded 3 marks.

1 Outline **three** reasons why Muslims do not accept euthanasia. (3 marks)

Hints
You could state a religious teaching in your answer. You can do this either by quoting it directly (using speech marks to show it is a quotation) or by paraphrasing (putting it in your own words).

Had a go

Muslims do not accept euthanasia as they believe only Allah can decide when a person should die.

Muslims believe life is a test of faith and suffering has a purpose. **Suggested answer**

Muslims believe there are alternatives to euthanasia such as hospices.

18

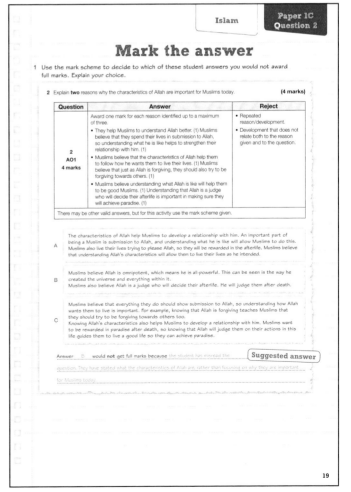

Islam — Paper 1C Question 2

Mark the answer

1 Use the mark scheme to decide to which of these student answers you would not award full marks. Explain your choice.

2 Explain **two** reasons why the characteristics of Allah are important for Muslims today. (4 marks)

Question	Answer	Reject
2 AO1 4 marks	Award one mark for each reason identified up to a maximum of three. • They help Muslims to understand Allah better. (1) Muslims believe that they spend their lives in submission to Allah, so understanding what he is like helps to strengthen their relationship with him. (1) • Muslims believe that the characteristics of Allah help them to follow how he wants them to live their lives. (1) Muslims believe that just as Allah is forgiving, they should also try to be forgiving towards others. (1) • Muslims believe understanding what Allah is like will help them to be good Muslims. (1) Understanding that Allah is a judge who will decide their afterlife is important in making sure they will achieve paradise. (1)	• Repeated reason/development. • Development that does not relate both to the reason given and to the question.
	There may be other valid answers, but for this activity use the mark scheme given.	

A The characteristics of Allah help Muslims to develop a relationship with him. An important part of being a Muslim is submission to Allah, and understanding what he is like will allow Muslims to do this. Muslims also live their lives trying to please Allah, so they will be rewarded in the afterlife. Muslims believe that understanding Allah's characteristics will allow them to live their lives as he intended.

B Muslims believe Allah is omnipotent, which means he is all-powerful. This can be seen in the way he created the universe and everything within it.
Muslims also believe Allah is a judge who will decide their afterlife. He will judge them after death.

C Muslims believe that everything they do should show submission to Allah, so understanding how Allah wants them to live is important. for example, knowing that Allah is forgiving teaches Muslims that they should try to be forgiving towards others too.
Knowing Allah's characteristics also helps Muslims to develop a relationship with him. Muslims want to be rewarded in paradise after death, so knowing that Allah will judge them on their actions in this life guides them to live a good life so they can achieve paradise.

Answer _____ B _____ would **not** get full marks **because** the student has misread the **Suggested answer**
question. They have stated what the characteristics of Allah are, rather than focusing on why they are important
for Muslims today.

19

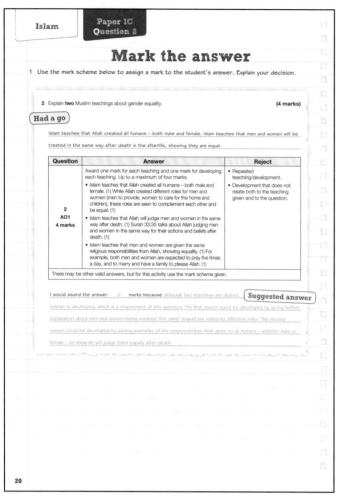

Islam — Paper 1C Question 2

Mark the answer

1 Use the mark scheme below to assign a mark to the student's answer. Explain your decision.

2 Explain **two** Muslim teachings about gender equality. **(4 marks)**

Had a go

Islam teaches that Allah created all humans – both male and female. Islam teaches that men and women will be treated in the same way after death in the afterlife, showing they are equal.

Question	Answer	Reject
2 AO1 4 marks	Award one mark for each teaching and one mark for developing each teaching. Up to a maximum of four marks. • Islam teaches that Allah created all humans – both male and female. (1) While Allah created different roles for men and women (men to provide, women to care for the home and children), these roles are seen to complement each other and be equal. (1) • Islam teaches that Allah will judge men and women in the same way after death. (1) Surah 33:35 talks about Allah judging men and women in the same way for their actions and beliefs after death. (1) • Islam teaches that men and women are given the same religious responsibilities from Allah, showing equality. (1) For example, both men and women are expected to pray five times a day, and to marry and have a family to please Allah. (1) There may be other valid answers, but for this activity use the mark scheme given.	• Repeated teaching/development. • Development that does not relate both to the teaching given and to the question.

I would award the answer **2** marks because although two teachings are stated, neither is developed, which is a requirement of this question. The first reason could be developed by giving further explanation about men and women being created 'the same' (equal) but suited to different roles. The second reason could be developed by adding examples of the responsibilities Allah gives to all humans – whether male or female – to show he will judge them equally after death. *Suggested answer*

20

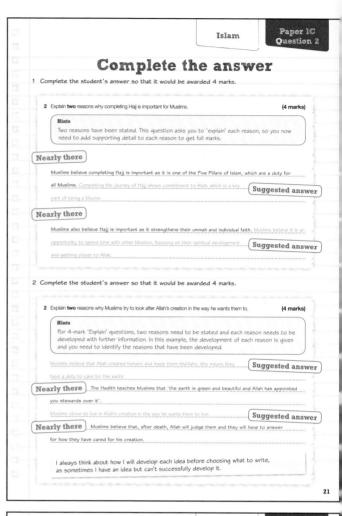

Islam — Paper 1C Question 2

Complete the answer

1 Complete the student's answer so that it would be awarded 4 marks.

2 Explain **two** reasons why completing Hajj is important for Muslims. **(4 marks)**

Hints
Two reasons have been stated. This question asks you to 'explain' each reason, so you now need to add supporting detail to each reason to get full marks.

Nearly there

Muslims believe completing Hajj is important as it is one of the Five Pillars of Islam, which are a duty for all Muslims. Completing the journey of Hajj shows commitment to Allah, which is a key part of being a Muslim. *Suggested answer*

Nearly there

Muslims also believe Hajj is important as it strengthens their ummah and individual faith. Muslims believe it is an opportunity to spend time with other Muslims, focusing on their spiritual development and getting closer to Allah. *Suggested answer*

2 Complete the student's answer so that it would be awarded 4 marks.

2 Explain **two** reasons why Muslims try to look after Allah's creation in the way he wants them to. **(4 marks)**

Hints
For 4-mark 'Explain' questions, two reasons need to be stated and each reason needs to be developed with further information. In this example, the development of each reason is given and you need to identify the reasons that have been developed.

Muslims believe that Allah created humans and made them khalifahs; this means they have a duty to care for the earth. *Suggested answer*

Nearly there The Hadith teaches Muslims that 'the earth is green and beautiful and Allah has appointed you stewards over it'.

Muslim strive to live in Allah's creation in the way he wants them to live. *Suggested answer*

Nearly there Muslims believe that, after death, Allah will judge them and they will have to answer for how they have cared for his creation.

I always think about how I will develop each idea before choosing what to write, as sometimes I have an idea but can't successfully develop it.

21

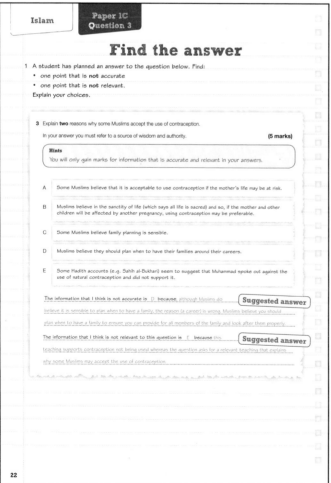

Islam — Paper 1C Question 3

Find the answer

1 A student has planned an answer to the question below. Find:
- one point that is **not** accurate
- one point that is **not** relevant.

Explain your choices.

3 Explain **two** reasons why some Muslims accept the use of contraception.

In your answer you must refer to a source of wisdom and authority. **(5 marks)**

Hints
You will only gain marks for information that is accurate and relevant in your answers.

A	Some Muslims believe that it is acceptable to use contraception if the mother's life may be at risk.
B	Muslims believe in the sanctity of life (which says all life is sacred) and so, if the mother and other children will be affected by another pregnancy, using contraception may be preferable.
C	Some Muslims believe family planning is sensible.
D	Muslims believe they should plan when to have their families around their careers.
E	Some Hadith accounts (e.g. Sahih al-Bukhari) seem to suggest that Muhammad spoke out against the use of natural contraception and did not support it.

The information that I think is not accurate is D because, although Muslims do believe it is sensible to plan when to have a family, the reason (a career) is wrong. Muslims believe you should plan when to have a family to ensure you can provide for all members of the family and look after them properly. *Suggested answer*

The information that I think is not relevant to this question is E because this teaching supports contraception not being used whereas the question asks for a relevant teaching that explains why some Muslims may accept the use of contraception. *Suggested answer*

22

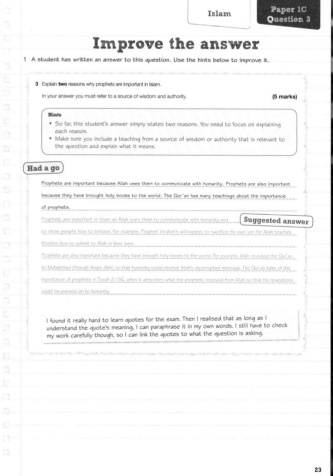

Islam — Paper 1C Question 3

Improve the answer

1 A student has written an answer to this question. Use the hints below to improve it.

3 Explain **two** reasons why prophets are important in Islam.

In your answer you must refer to a source of wisdom and authority. **(5 marks)**

Hints
- So far, this student's answer simply states two reasons. You need to focus on explaining each reason.
- Make sure you include a teaching from a source of wisdom or authority that is relevant to the question and explain what it means.

Had a go

Prophets are important because Allah uses them to communicate with humanity. Prophets are also important because they have brought holy books to the world. The Qur'an has many teachings about the importance of prophets.

Prophets are important in Islam as Allah uses them to communicate with humanity and to show people how to behave. For example, Prophet Ibrahim's willingness to sacrifice his own son for Allah teaches Muslims how to submit to Allah in their lives. *Suggested answer*

Prophets are also important because they have brought holy books to the world. For example, Allah revealed the Qur'an to Muhammad through Angel Jibril, so that humanity could receive Allah's uncorrupted message. The Qur'an talks of the importance of prophets in Surah 2:136, when it describes what the prophets received from Allah so that his revelations could be passed on to humanity.

I found it really hard to learn quotes for the exam. Then I realised that as long as I understand the quote's meaning, I can paraphrase it in my own words. I still have to check my work carefully though, so I can link the quotes to what the question is asking.

23

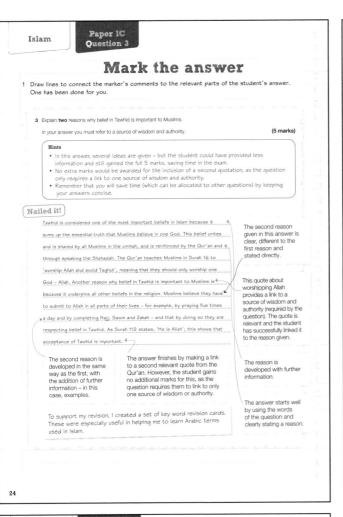

Islam — Paper 1C Question 3

Mark the answer

1 Draw lines to connect the marker's comments to the relevant parts of the student's answer. One has been done for you.

3 Explain **two** reasons why belief in Tawhid is important to Muslims.

In your answer you must refer to a source of wisdom and authority. **(5 marks)**

Hints
- In this answer, several ideas are given – but the student could have provided less information and still gained the full 5 marks, saving time in the exam.
- No extra marks would be awarded for the inclusion of a second quotation, as the question only requires a link to one source of wisdom and authority.
- Remember that you will save time (which can be allocated to other questions) by keeping your answers concise.

Nailed it!

Tawhid is considered one of the most important beliefs in Islam because it sums up the essential truth that Muslims believe in one God. This belief unites and is shared by all Muslims in the ummah, and is reinforced by the Qur'an and through speaking the Shahadah. The Qur'an teaches Muslims in Surah 16 to 'worship Allah and avoid Taghut', meaning that they should only worship one God – Allah. Another reason why belief in Tawhid is important to Muslims is because it underpins all other beliefs in the religion. Muslims believe they have to submit to Allah in all parts of their lives – for example, by praying five times a day and by completing Hajj, Sawm and Zakah – and that by doing so they are respecting belief in Tawhid. As Surah 112 states, 'He is Allah'; this shows that acceptance of Tawhid is important.

To support my revision, I created a set of key word revision cards. These were especially useful in helping me to learn Arabic terms used in Islam.

Marker's comments:
- The second reason given in this answer is clear, different to the first reason and stated directly.
- This quote about worshipping Allah provides a link to a source of wisdom and authority (required by the question). The quote is relevant and the student has successfully linked it to the reason given.
- The reason is developed with further information.
- The answer starts well by using the words of the question and clearly stating a reason.
- The second reason is developed in the same way as the first, with the addition of further information – in this case, examples.
- The answer finishes by making a link to a second relevant quote from the Qur'an. However, the student gains no additional marks for this, as the question requires them to link to only one source of wisdom or authority.

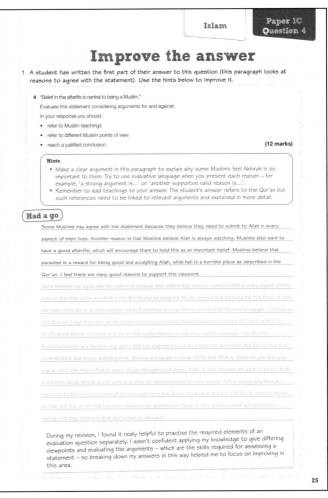

Islam — Paper 1C Question 4

Improve the answer

1 A student has written the first part of their answer to this question (this paragraph looks at reasons to agree with the statement). Use the hints below to improve it.

4 "Belief in the afterlife is central to being a Muslim."

Evaluate this statement considering arguments for and against.

In your response you should:
- refer to Muslim teachings
- refer to different Muslim points of view
- reach a justified conclusion. **(12 marks)**

Hints
- Make a clear argument in this paragraph to explain why some Muslims feel Akhirah is so important to them. Try to use evaluative language when you present each reason – for example, 'a strong argument is...' or 'another supportive valid reason is...'.
- Remember to add teachings to your answer. The student's answer refers to the Qur'an but such references need to be linked to relevant arguments and explained in more detail.

Had a go

Some Muslims may agree with the statement because they believe they need to submit to Allah in every aspect of their lives. Another reason is that Muslims believe Allah is always watching. Muslims also want to have a good afterlife, which will encourage them to hold this as an important belief. Muslims believe that paradise is a reward for being good and accepting Allah, while hell is a horrible place as described in the Qur'an. I feel there are many good reasons to support this viewpoint.

Some Muslims may agree with the statement because they believe they need to submit to Allah in every aspect of their lives, so that they will be with Allah in the afterlife and be rewarded. Muslims believe that following the Five Pillars of Islam, the rules in the Qur'an and the example set by Muhammad will help them to please Allah. Muslims are taught in the Qur'an that Allah will judge them after death on their actions, and knowing this will happen means they will listen carefully to beliefs about Akhirah to ensure they live in a way Allah wants them to so that they stay to be rewarded in the afterlife. A second reason why Muslims may agree with the statement is because they are aware from the Qur'an that Allah is omnipotent and always watching them. Muslims are taught in Surah 50:16 that 'Allah is closer to you than your jugular vein'; this means Allah is aware of your thoughts and deeds. If this is true, Muslims will want to please Allah and beliefs about Akhirah will be central as they will determine how Muslims behave. A final reason why Akhirah is important to Muslims is because of the descriptions in the Qur'an of paradise and hell. The Qur'an teaches Muslims to 'fear the fire of hell that has been prepared for disbelievers (Surah 3:131), and this belief will be central in making sure they believe in Allah and behave as he wants.

During my revision, I found it really helpful to practise the required elements of an evaluation question separately. I wasn't confident applying my knowledge to give differing viewpoints and evaluating the arguments – which are the skills required for assessing a statement – so breaking down my answers in this way helped me to focus on improving in this area.

Islam — Paper 1C Question 4

Mark the answer

1 Draw lines to connect the marker's comments to the relevant parts of the answer. One has been done for you.

4 "Muslim beliefs about the creation of the universe are in conflict with scientific beliefs."

Evaluate this statement considering arguments for and against.

In your response you should:
- refer to Muslim teachings
- refer to different Muslim points of view
- reach a justified conclusion. **(12 marks)**

Hints
Use the bulleted list in the 12-mark 'Evaluate' question as a checklist to ensure you have included all the required elements in your answer.

Nearly there

Some Muslims may strongly agree with the statement, believing that only what is written in the Qur'an is true about the creation of the universe, as the Qur'an contains the words of Allah. The Qur'an says Allah created the universe and science says it was the Big Bang; these religious and scientific accounts are very different, so they are in conflict. Another reason to agree with the statement is that science appears to suggest the universe was created by chance, while Islam teaches that Allah planned it. Although there is some good evidence for this view, I feel that it is difficult to reject science in today's modern world. Therefore, there are probably other arguments that are stronger. On the other hand, many Muslims believe science and Islam are not in conflict over the creation of the universe. They believe that science is actually part of Allah's plan in creating the universe, and that science helps them to understand better how Allah planned and made his creation. If this view is accepted, there is no conflict between Islam and science – they are in fact seen to work together. Moreover, there are some teachings in the Qur'an that Muslims point to as possibly discussing the role of science in creating the universe. This adds further evidence to the view that there is no conflict between science and religion overall. Having considered all the arguments carefully, I have to conclude that I disagree with the statement more than I agree with it. I feel that, in today's scientific world, it is more acceptable for Muslims to look for ways of making science and Islam work together to explain the creation of the universe, rather than for these different scientific and religious accounts to be in conflict.

Marker's comments:
- There is some consideration of why the point of view is valid. This approach should be applied consistently throughout the answer.
- There is a successful change of argument at this point – the student goes on to explain reasons to disagree with the statement.
- The answer starts with a clear focus by identifying arguments to agree with the statement.
- The answer offers a justified conclusion at the end, once all the arguments have been considered.
- The student has mentioned a source of authority, but no quotes or explanation are used.
- Although the answer offers a conclusion, it would be stronger if the student had identified some of the more persuasive arguments and explained more clearly how they reached their conclusion.

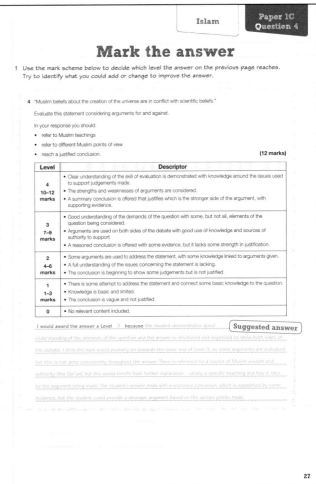

Islam — Paper 1C Question 4

Mark the answer

1 Use the mark scheme below to decide which level the answer on the previous page reaches. Try to identify what you could add or change to improve the answer.

4 "Muslim beliefs about the creation of the universe are in conflict with scientific beliefs."

Evaluate this statement considering arguments for and against.

In your response you should:
- refer to Muslim teachings
- refer to different Muslim points of view
- reach a justified conclusion. **(12 marks)**

Level	Descriptor
4 **10–12 marks**	• Clear understanding of the skill of evaluation is demonstrated with knowledge around the issues used to support judgements made. • The strengths and weaknesses of arguments are considered. • A summary conclusion is offered that justifies which is the stronger side of the argument, with supporting evidence.
3 **7–9 marks**	• Good understanding of the demands of the question with some, but not all, elements of the question being considered. • Arguments are used on both sides of the debate with good use of knowledge and sources of authority to support. • A reasoned conclusion is offered with some evidence, but it lacks some strength in justification.
2 **4–6 marks**	• Some arguments are used to address the statement, with some knowledge linked to arguments given. • A full understanding of the issues concerning the statement is lacking. • The conclusion is beginning to show some judgements but is not justified.
1 **1–3 marks**	• There is some attempt to address the statement and connect some basic knowledge to the question. • Knowledge is basic and limited. • The conclusion is vague and not justified.
0	• No relevant content included.

Suggested answer

I would award the answer a Level 3 because the student demonstrates good understanding of the demands of the question and the answer is structured and organised to show both sides of the debate. I think the mark would probably be towards the lower end of Level 3, as some arguments are evaluated, but this is not done consistently throughout the answer. There is reference to a source of Muslim wisdom and authority (the Qur'an), but this would benefit from further explanation – ideally a specific teaching and how it links to the argument being made. The student's answer ends with a reasoned conclusion, which is supported by some evidence, but the student could provide a stronger argument based on the various points made.

Answers

Panel 1 (top-left)

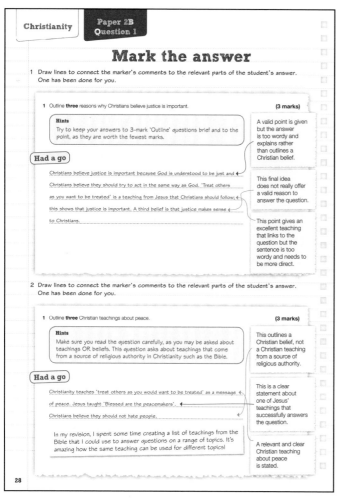

Christianity — Paper 2B Question 1

Mark the answer

1 Draw lines to connect the marker's comments to the relevant parts of the student's answer. One has been done for you.

1 Outline **three** reasons why Christians believe justice is important. (3 marks)

Hints
Try to keep your answers to 3-mark 'Outline' questions brief and to the point, as they are worth the fewest marks.

Had a go

Christians believe justice is important because God is understood to be just and Christians believe they should try to act in the same way as God. 'Treat others as you want to be treated' is a teaching from Jesus that Christians should follow; this shows that justice is important. A third belief is that justice makes sense to Christians.

- A valid point is given but the answer is too wordy and explains rather than outlines a Christian belief.
- This final idea does not really offer a valid reason to answer the question.
- This point gives an excellent teaching that links to the question but the sentence is too wordy and needs to be more direct.

2 Draw lines to connect the marker's comments to the relevant parts of the student's answer. One has been done for you.

1 Outline **three** Christian teachings about peace. (3 marks)

Hints
Make sure you read the question carefully, as you may be asked about teachings OR beliefs. This question asks about teachings that come from a source of religious authority in Christianity such as the Bible.

Had a go

Christianity teaches 'treat others as you would want to be treated' as a message of peace. Jesus taught 'Blessed are the peacemakers'. Christians believe they should not hate people.

In my revision, I spent some time creating a list of teachings from the Bible that I could use to answer questions on a range of topics. It's amazing how the same teaching can be used for different topics!

- This outlines a Christian belief, not a Christian teaching from a source of religious authority.
- This is a clear statement about one of Jesus' teachings that successfully answers the question.
- A relevant and clear Christian teaching about peace is stated.

28

Panel 2 (top-right)

Christianity — Paper 2B Question 1

Complete the question

1 Use the student's answer to complete the question.

Hints
Completing a task like this, where you need to identify the question, will help you to understand whether your answer focuses on what is being asked. With 'Outline' questions, it is important to give short, direct and straightforward answers.

1 Outline **three** ways the Church can support people in the local community. (3 marks)

Nailed it! **Suggested answer**

The Church can hold coffee mornings. The Church can also organise a youth club for children to attend. The Church may organise food banks.

I found it useful to create my own examples of questions as part of my revision. This really helped me to understand what the examiner is looking for.

2 Use the student's answer to complete the question.

1 Outline **three** Christian beliefs about the Trinity. (3 marks)

Nailed it! **Suggested answer**

The Trinity helps Christians to understand the nature of God. It is the idea of God as Father, Son and Holy Spirit. It shows Christians that the three parts are equally important.

3 Use the student's answer to complete the question.

1 Outline **three** ways Christians celebrate Christmas. (3 marks)

Nailed it! **Suggested answer**

Christians send cards and give presents. They may attend Midnight Mass. They may also put on a nativity play.

Hints
Remember that there are many possible answers to the 3-mark 'Outline' questions. You are simply required to identify three correct ideas.

4 Use the student's answer to complete the question.

1 Outline **three** conditions of Just War theory. (3 marks)

Nailed it! **Suggested answer**

One condition is that there must be a reasonable chance of success. Another condition is that it must be used only as a last resort. A third condition is that its aim must be to bring about peace.

29

Panel 3 (bottom-left)

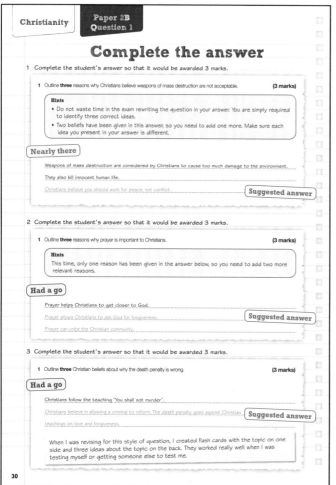

Christianity — Paper 2B Question 1

Complete the answer

1 Complete the student's answer so that it would be awarded 3 marks.

1 Outline **three** reasons why Christians believe weapons of mass destruction are not acceptable. (3 marks)

Hints
- Do not waste time in the exam rewriting the question in your answer. You are simply required to identify three correct ideas.
- Two beliefs have been given in this answer, so you need to add one more. Make sure each idea you present in your answer is different.

Nearly there

Weapons of mass destruction are considered by Christians to cause too much damage to the environment. They also kill innocent human life. Christians believe you should work for peace, not conflict. **Suggested answer**

2 Complete the student's answer so that it would be awarded 3 marks.

1 Outline **three** reasons why prayer is important to Christians. (3 marks)

Hints
This time, only one reason has been given in the answer below, so you need to add two more relevant reasons.

Had a go

Prayer helps Christians to get closer to God. Prayer allows Christians to ask God for forgiveness. Prayer can unite the Christian community. **Suggested answer**

3 Complete the student's answer so that it would be awarded 3 marks.

1 Outline **three** Christian beliefs about why the death penalty is wrong. (3 marks)

Had a go

Christians follow the teaching 'You shall not murder'. Christians believe in allowing a criminal to reform. The death penalty goes against Christian teachings on love and forgiveness. **Suggested answer**

When I was revising for this style of question, I created flash cards with the topic on one side and three ideas about the topic on the back. They worked really well when I was testing myself or getting someone else to test me.

30

Panel 4 (bottom-right)

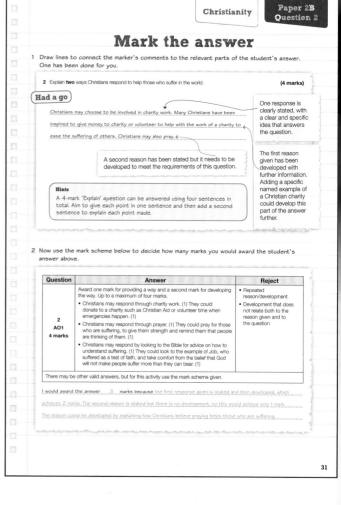

Christianity — Paper 2B Question 2

Mark the answer

1 Draw lines to connect the marker's comments to the relevant parts of the student's answer. One has been done for you.

2 Explain **two** ways Christians respond to help those who suffer in the world. (4 marks)

Had a go

Christians may choose to be involved in charity work. Many Christians have been inspired to give money to charity or volunteer to help with the work of a charity to ease the suffering of others. Christians may also pray.

- One response is clearly stated, with a clear and specific idea that answers the question.
- A second reason has been stated but it needs to be developed to meet the requirements of this question.
- The first reason given has been developed with further information. Adding a specific named example of a Christian charity could develop this part of the answer further.

Hints
A 4-mark 'Explain' question can be answered using four sentences in total. Aim to give each point in one sentence and then add a second sentence to explain each point made.

2 Now use the mark scheme below to decide how many marks you would award the student's answer above.

Question	Answer	Reject
2 AO1 4 marks	Award one mark for providing a way and a second mark for developing the way. Up to a maximum of four marks. • Christians may respond through charity work. (1) They could donate to a charity such as Christian Aid or volunteer time when emergencies happen. (1) • Christians may respond through prayer. (1) They could pray for those who are suffering, to give them strength and remind them that people are thinking of them. (1) • Christians may respond by looking to the Bible for advice on how to understand suffering. (1) They could look to the example of Job, who suffered as a test of faith, and take comfort from the belief that God will not make people suffer more than they can bear. (1)	• Repeated reason/development • Development that does not relate both to the reason given and to the question

There may be other valid answers, but for this activity use the mark scheme given.

I would award the answer 3 marks because the first response given is stated and then developed, which achieves 2 marks. The second reason is stated but there is no development, so this would achieve only 1 mark. The reason could be developed by explaining how Christians believe praying helps those who are suffering.

31

82

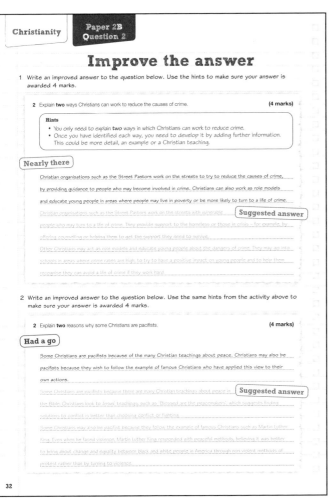

Christianity — Paper 2B Question 2

Improve the answer

1 Write an improved answer to the question below. Use the hints to make sure your answer is awarded 4 marks.

2 Explain **two** ways Christians can work to reduce the causes of crime. **(4 marks)**

Hints
- You only need to explain **two** ways in which Christians can work to reduce crime.
- Once you have identified each way, you need to develop it by adding further information. This could be more detail, an example or a Christian teaching.

Nearly there

Christian organisations such as the Street Pastors work on the streets to try to reduce the causes of crime, by providing guidance to people who may become involved in crime. Christians can also work as role models and educate young people in areas where people may live in poverty or be more likely to turn to a life of crime.

Suggested answer
Christian organisations such as the Street Pastors work on the streets with vulnerable people who may turn to a life of crime. They provide support to the homeless or those in crisis – for example, by offering counselling or helping them to get the support they need to survive.

Other Christians may act as role models and educate young people about the dangers of crime. They may go into schools in areas where crime rates are high, to try to have a positive impact on young people and to help them recognise they can avoid a life of crime if they work hard.

2 Write an improved answer to the question below. Use the same hints from the activity above to make sure your answer is awarded 4 marks.

2 Explain **two** reasons why some Christians are pacifists. **(4 marks)**

Had a go

Some Christians are pacifists because of the many Christian teachings about peace. Christians may also be pacifists because they wish to follow the example of famous Christians who have applied this view to their own actions.

Suggested answer
Some Christians are pacifists because there are many Christian teachings about peace in the Bible. Christians look to Jesus' teachings, such as 'Blessed are the peacemakers', which suggests finding solutions to conflict is better than choosing conflict or fighting.

Some Christians may also be pacifist because they follow the example of famous Christians such as Martin Luther King. Even when he faced violence, Martin Luther King responded with peaceful methods, believing it was better to bring about change and equality between black and white people in America through non-violent methods of protest rather than by turning to violence.

32

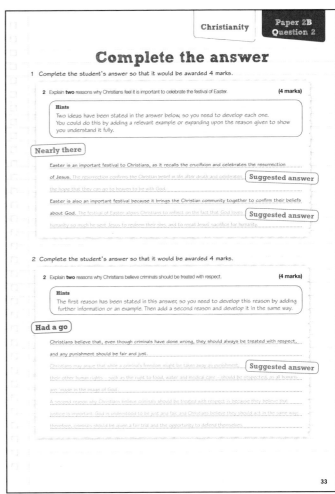

Christianity — Paper 2B Question 2

Complete the answer

1 Complete the student's answer so that it would be awarded 4 marks.

2 Explain **two** reasons why Christians feel it is important to celebrate the festival of Easter. **(4 marks)**

Hints
Two ideas have been stated in the answer below, so you need to develop each one.
You could do this by adding a relevant example or expanding upon the reason given to show you understand it fully.

Nearly there

Easter is an important festival to Christians, as it recalls the crucifixion and celebrates the resurrection of Jesus. **Suggested answer** The resurrection confirms the Christian belief in life after death and celebrates the hope that they can go to heaven to be with God.

Easter is also an important festival because it brings the Christian community together to confirm their beliefs about God. **Suggested answer** The festival of Easter allows Christians to reflect on the fact that God loves humanity so much he sent Jesus to redeem their sins, and to recall Jesus' sacrifice for humanity.

2 Complete the student's answer so that it would be awarded 4 marks.

2 Explain **two** reasons why Christians believe criminals should be treated with respect. **(4 marks)**

Hints
The first reason has been stated in this answer, so you need to develop this reason by adding further information or an example. Then add a second reason and develop it in the same way.

Had a go

Christians believe that, even though criminals have done wrong, they should always be treated with respect, and any punishment should be fair and just.

Suggested answer
Christians may argue that, while a criminal's freedom might be taken away in punishment, their other human rights – such as the right to food, water and medical care – should be respected, as all humans are made in the image of God.

A second reason why Christians believe criminals should be treated with respect is because they believe that justice is important. God is understood to be just and fair and Christians believe they should act in the same way; therefore, criminals should be given a fair trial and the opportunity to defend themselves.

33

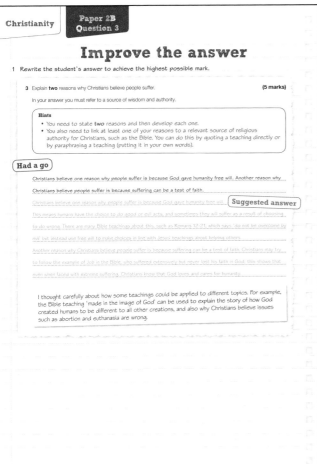

Christianity — Paper 2B Question 3

Improve the answer

1 Rewrite the student's answer to achieve the highest possible mark.

3 Explain **two** reasons why Christians believe people suffer. **(5 marks)**

In your answer you must refer to a source of wisdom and authority.

Hints
- You need to state **two** reasons and then develop each one.
- You also need to link at least one of your reasons to a relevant source of religious authority for Christians, such as the Bible. You can do this by quoting a teaching directly or by paraphrasing a teaching (putting it in your own words).

Had a go

Christians believe one reason why people suffer is because God gave humanity free will. Another reason why Christians believe people suffer is because suffering can be a test of faith.

Suggested answer
Christians believe one reason why people suffer is because God gave humanity free will. This means humans have the choice to do good or evil acts, and sometimes they will suffer as a result of choosing to do wrong. There are many Bible teachings about this, such as Romans 12:21, which says, 'do not be overcome by evil' but instead use free will to make choices in line with Jesus' teachings about helping others.

Another reason why Christians believe people suffer is because suffering can be a test of faith. Christians may try to follow the example of Job in the Bible, who suffered extensively but never lost his faith in God; this shows that even when faced with extreme suffering, Christians know that God loves and cares for humanity.

I thought carefully about how some teachings could be applied to different topics. For example, the Bible teaching 'made in the image of God' can be used to explain the story of how God created humans to be different to all other creations, and also why Christians believe issues such as abortion and euthanasia are wrong.

34

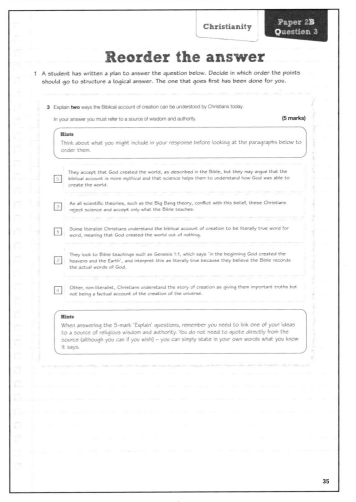

Christianity — Paper 2B Question 3

Reorder the answer

1 A student has written a plan to answer the question below. Decide in which order the points should go to structure a logical answer. The one that goes first has been done for you.

3 Explain **two** ways the Biblical account of creation can be understood by Christians today.

In your answer you must refer to a source of wisdom and authority. **(5 marks)**

Hints
Think about what you might include in your response before looking at the paragraphs below to order them.

5 They accept that God created the world, as described in the Bible, but they may argue that the biblical account is more mythical and that science helps them to understand how God was able to create the world.

3 As all scientific theories, such as the Big Bang theory, conflict with this belief, these Christians reject science and accept only what the Bible teaches.

1 Some literalist Christians understand the biblical account of creation to be literally true word for word, meaning that God created the world out of nothing.

2 They look to Bible teachings such as Genesis 1:1, which says 'in the beginning God created the heavens and the Earth', and interpret this as literally true because they believe the Bible records the actual words of God.

4 Other, non-literalist, Christians understand the story of creation as giving them important truths but not being a factual account of the creation of the universe.

Hints
When answering the 5-mark 'Explain' questions, remember you need to link one of your ideas to a source of religious wisdom and authority. You do not need to quote directly from the source (although you can if you wish) – you can simply state in your own words what you know it says.

35

Answers

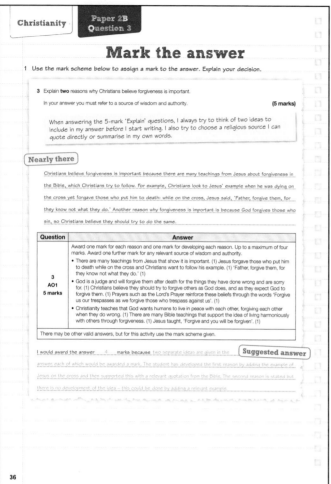

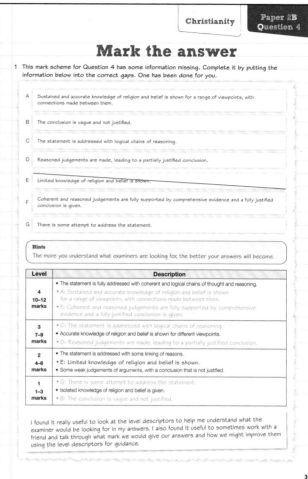

Christianity — Paper 2B Question 3

Mark the answer

1 Use the mark scheme below to assign a mark to the answer. Explain your decision.

> 3 Explain **two** reasons why Christians believe forgiveness is important.
>
> In your answer you must refer to a source of wisdom and authority.
>
> (5 marks)

> When answering the 5-mark 'Explain' questions, I always try to think of two ideas to include in my answer *before* I start writing. I also try to choose a religious source I can quote directly or summarise in my own words.

Nearly there

Christians believe forgiveness is important because there are many teachings from Jesus about forgiveness in the Bible, which Christians try to follow. For example, Christians look to Jesus' example when he was dying on the cross, yet forgave those who put him to death: while on the cross, Jesus said, 'Father, forgive them, for they know not what they do.' Another reason why forgiveness is important is because God forgives those who sin, so Christians believe they should try to do the same.

Question	Answer
3 AO1 5 marks	Award one mark for each reason and one mark for developing each reason. Up to a maximum of four marks. Award one further mark for any relevant source of wisdom and authority. • There are many teachings from Jesus that show it is important. (1) Jesus forgave those who put him to death while on the cross and Christians want to follow his example. (1) 'Father, forgive them, for they know not what they do.' (1) • God is a judge and will forgive them after death for the things they have done wrong and are sorry for. (1) Christians believe they should try to forgive others as God does, and as they expect God to forgive them. (1) Prayers such as the Lord's Prayer reinforce these beliefs through the words 'Forgive us our trespasses as we forgive those who trespass against us'. (1) • Christianity teaches that God wants humans to live in peace with each other, forgiving each other when they do wrong. (1) There are many Bible teachings that support the idea of living harmoniously with others through forgiveness. (1) Jesus taught, 'Forgive and you will be forgiven'. (1)

There may be other valid answers, but for this activity use the mark scheme given.

I would award the answer ___4___ marks because two separate ideas are given in the **Suggested answer** answer each of which would be awarded a mark. The student has developed the first reason by adding the example of Jesus on the cross and then supported this with a relevant quotation from the Bible. The second reason is stated but there is no development of the idea – this could be done by adding a relevant example.

36

Christianity — Paper 2B Question 4

Mark the answer

1 This mark scheme for Question 4 has some information missing. Complete it by putting the information below into the correct gaps. One has been done for you.

A	Sustained and accurate knowledge of religion and belief is shown for a range of viewpoints, with connections made between them.
B	The conclusion is vague and not justified.
C	The statement is addressed with logical chains of reasoning.
D	Reasoned judgements are made, leading to a partially justified conclusion.
E	Limited knowledge of religion and belief is shown.
F	Coherent and reasoned judgements are fully supported by comprehensive evidence and a fully justified conclusion is given.
G	There is some attempt to address the statement.

> **Hints**
> The more you understand what examiners are looking for, the better your answers will become.

Level	Description
4 10–12 marks	• The statement is fully addressed with coherent and logical chains of thought and reasoning. • A: Sustained and accurate knowledge of religion and belief is shown for a range of viewpoints, with connections made between them. • F: Coherent and reasoned judgements are fully supported by comprehensive evidence and a fully justified conclusion is given.
3 7–9 marks	• C: The statement is addressed with logical chains of reasoning. • Accurate knowledge of religion and belief is shown for different viewpoints. • D: Reasoned judgements are made, leading to a partially justified conclusion.
2 4–6 marks	• The statement is addressed with some linking of reasons. • E: Limited knowledge of religion and belief is shown. • Some weak judgements of arguments, with a conclusion that is not justified.
1 1–3 marks	• G: There is some attempt to address the statement. • Isolated knowledge of religion and belief is shown. • B: The conclusion is vague and not justified.

I found it really useful to look at the level descriptors to help me understand what the examiner would be looking for in my answers. I also found it useful to sometimes work with a friend and talk through what mark we would give our answers and how we might improve them using the level descriptors for guidance.

37

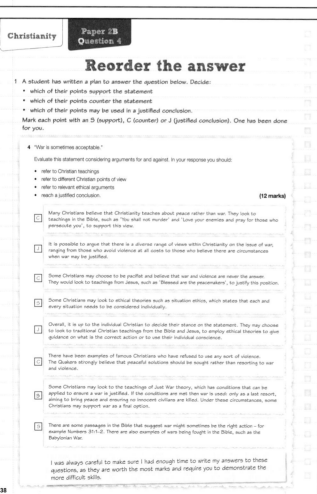

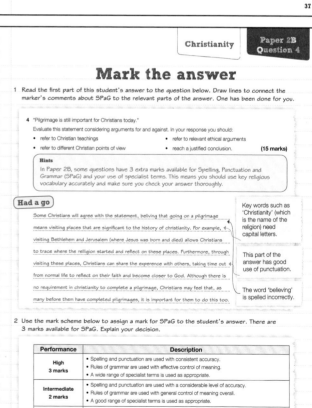

Christianity — Paper 2B Question 4

Reorder the answer

1 A student has written a plan to answer the question below. Decide:
- which of their points support the statement
- which of their points counter the statement
- which of their points may be used in a justified conclusion.

Mark each point with an S (support), C (counter) or J (justified conclusion). One has been done for you.

> 4 "War is sometimes acceptable."
>
> Evaluate this statement considering arguments for and against. In your response you should:
> - refer to Christian teachings
> - refer to different Christian points of view
> - refer to relevant ethical arguments
> - reach a justified conclusion.
>
> (12 marks)

C	Many Christians believe that Christianity teaches about peace rather than war. They look to teachings in the Bible, such as 'You shall not murder' and 'Love your enemies and pray for those who persecute you', to support this view.
J	It is possible to argue that there is a diverse range of views within Christianity on the issue of war, ranging from those who avoid violence at all costs to those who believe there are circumstances when war may be justified.
C	Some Christians may choose to be pacifist and believe that war and violence are never the answer. They would look to teachings from Jesus, such as 'Blessed are the peacemakers', to justify this position.
S	Some Christians may look to ethical theories such as situation ethics, which states that each and every situation needs to be considered individually.
J	Overall, it is up to the individual Christian to decide their stance on the statement. They may choose to look to traditional Christian teachings from the Bible and Jesus, to employ ethical theories to give guidance on what is the correct action or to use their individual conscience.
C	There have been examples of famous Christians who have refused to use any sort of violence. The Quakers strongly believe that peaceful solutions should be sought rather than resorting to war and violence.
S	Some Christians may look to the teachings of Just War theory, which has conditions that can be applied to ensure a war is justified. If the conditions are met then war is used: only as a last resort, aiming to bring peace and ensuring no innocent civilians are killed. Under these circumstances, some Christians may support war as a final option.
S	There are some passages in the Bible that suggest war might sometimes be the right action – for example Numbers 31:1–2. There are also examples of wars being fought in the Bible, such as the Babylonian War.

> I was always careful to make sure I had enough time to write my answers to these questions, as they are worth the most marks and require you to demonstrate the more difficult skills.

38

Christianity — Paper 2B Question 4

Mark the answer

1 Read the first part of this student's answer to the question below. Draw lines to connect the marker's comments about SPaG to the relevant parts of the answer. One has been done for you.

> 4 "Pilgrimage is still important for Christians today."
>
> Evaluate this statement considering arguments for and against. In your response you should:
> - refer to Christian teachings
> - refer to different Christian points of view
> - refer to relevant ethical arguments
> - reach a justified conclusion.
>
> (15 marks)

> **Hints**
> In Paper 2B, some questions have 3 extra marks available for Spelling, Punctuation and Grammar (SPaG) and your use of specialist terms. This means you should use key religious vocabulary accurately and make sure you check your answer thoroughly.

Had a go

Some Christians will agree with the statement, believing that going on a pilgrimage means visiting places that are significant to the history of christianity. For example, visiting Bethlehem and Jerusalem (where Jesus was born and died) allows Christians to trace where the religion started and reflect on these places. Furthermore, through visiting these places, Christians can share the experience with others, taking time out from normal life to reflect on their faith and become closer to God. Although there is no requirement in christianity to complete a pilgrimage, Christians may feel that, as many before them have completed pilgrimages, it is important for them to do this too.

- Key words such as 'Christianity' (which is the name of the religion) need capital letters.
- This part of the answer has good use of punctuation.
- The word 'believing' is spelled incorrectly.

2 Use the mark scheme below to assign a mark for SPaG to the student's answer. There are 3 marks available for SPaG. Explain your decision.

Performance	Description
High 3 marks	• Spelling and punctuation are used with consistent accuracy. • Rules of grammar are used with effective control of meaning. • A wide range of specialist terms is used as appropriate.
Intermediate 2 marks	• Spelling and punctuation are used with a considerable level of accuracy. • Rules of grammar are used with general control of meaning overall. • A good range of specialist terms is used as appropriate.
Threshold 1 mark	• Spelling and punctuation are used with a reasonable level of accuracy. • Rules of grammar are used with some control of meaning and errors do not significantly hinder meaning overall. • A limited range of specialist terms is used as appropriate.
No marks awarded	• Nothing is written or the response does not relate to the question. • Errors in spelling, punctuation and grammar make it very difficult to understand the answer.

I would give this answer ___2___ out of 3 marks because the student has used a good range of specialist terms appropriately and spelling and punctuation are used with a considerable level of accuracy.

39

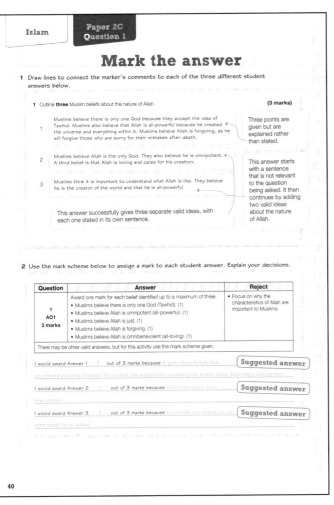

Islam — Paper 2C Question 1

Mark the answer

1 Draw lines to connect the marker's comments to each of the three different student answers below.

1 Outline **three** Muslim beliefs about the nature of Allah. **(3 marks)**

1 Muslims believe there is only one God because they accept the idea of Tawhid. Muslims also believe that Allah is all-powerful because he created the universe and everything within it. Muslims believe Allah is forgiving, as he will forgive those who are sorry for their mistakes after death.

Three points are given but are explained rather than stated.

2 Muslims believe Allah is the only God. They also believe he is omnipotent. A third belief is that Allah is loving and cares for his creation.

This answer starts with a sentence that is not relevant to the question being asked. It then continues by adding two valid ideas about the nature of Allah.

3 Muslims think it is important to understand what Allah is like. They believe he is the creator of the world and that he is all-powerful.

This answer successfully gives three separate valid ideas, with each one stated in its own sentence.

2 Use the mark scheme below to assign a mark to each student answer. Explain your decisions.

Question	Answer	Reject
1 AO1 3 marks	Award one mark for each belief identified up to a maximum of three. • Muslims believe there is only one God (Tawhid). (1) • Muslims believe Allah is omnipotent (all-powerful). (1) • Muslims believe Allah is just. (1) • Muslims believe Allah is forgiving. (1) • Muslims believe Allah is omnibenevolent (all-loving). (1)	• Focus on why the characteristics of Allah are important to Muslims.
	There may be other valid answers, but for this activity use the mark scheme given.	

I would award Answer 1 ___ out of 3 marks because it gives three beliefs that **Suggested answer** are relevant and valid. However, the student has wasted time explaining the beliefs rather than simply stating them.

I would award Answer 2 ___ out of 3 marks because three valid points have **Suggested answer** been stated.

I would award Answer 3 ___ out of 3 marks because two beliefs are stated, so one **Suggested answer** more needs to be added.

40

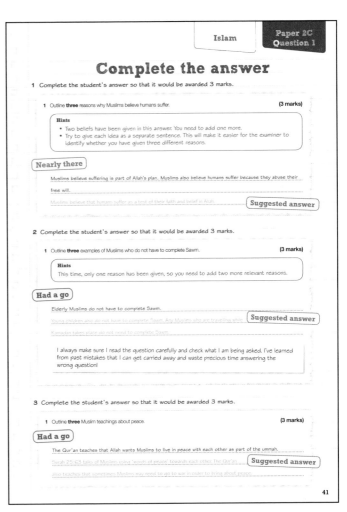

Islam — Paper 2C Question 1

Complete the answer

1 Complete the student's answer so that it would be awarded 3 marks.

1 Outline **three** reasons why Muslims believe humans suffer. **(3 marks)**

Hints
• Two beliefs have been given in this answer. You need to add one more.
• Try to give each idea as a separate sentence. This will make it easier for the examiner to identify whether you have given three different reasons.

Nearly there

Muslims believe suffering is part of Allah's plan. Muslims also believe humans suffer because they abuse their free will.

Muslims believe that humans suffer as a test of their faith and belief in Allah. **Suggested answer**

2 Complete the student's answer so that it would be awarded 3 marks.

1 Outline **three** examples of Muslims who do not have to complete Sawm. **(3 marks)**

Hints
This time, only one reason has been given, so you need to add two more relevant reasons.

Had a go

Elderly Muslims do not have to complete Sawm.

Young children also do not have to complete Sawm. Any Muslims who are travelling while **Suggested answer** Ramadan takes place do not need to complete Sawm.

I always make sure I read the question carefully and check what I am being asked. I've learned from past mistakes that I can get carried away and waste precious time answering the wrong question!

3 Complete the student's answer so that it would be awarded 3 marks.

1 Outline **three** Muslim teachings about peace. **(3 marks)**

Had a go

The Qur'an teaches that Allah wants Muslims to live in peace with each other as part of the ummah.

Surah 25:63 talks of Muslims voicing 'words of peace' towards each other. The Qur'an **Suggested answer** also teaches that sometimes Muslims may need to go to war in order to bring about peace.

41

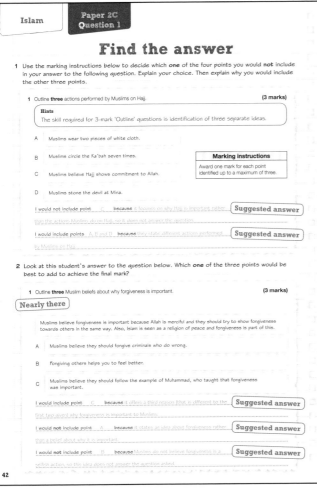

Islam — Paper 2C Question 1

Find the answer

1 Use the marking instructions below to decide which **one** of the four points you would **not** include in your answer to the following question. Explain your choice. Then explain why you would include the other three points.

1 Outline **three** actions performed by Muslims on Hajj. **(3 marks)**

Hints
The skill required for 3-mark 'Outline' questions is identification of three separate ideas.

A Muslims wear two pieces of white cloth.

B Muslims circle the Ka'bah seven times.

C Muslims believe Hajj shows commitment to Allah.

Marking instructions
Award one mark for each point identified up to a maximum of three.

D Muslims stone the devil at Mina.

I would not include point C because it focuses on why Hajj is important rather **Suggested answer** than the actions Muslims do on Hajj, so it does not answer the question.

I would include points A, B and D because they state different actions performed **Suggested answer** by Muslims on Hajj.

2 Look at this student's answer to the question below. Which **one** of the three points would be best to add to achieve the final mark?

1 Outline **three** Muslim beliefs about why forgiveness is important. **(3 marks)**

Nearly there

Muslims believe forgiveness is important because Allah is merciful and they should try to show forgiveness towards others in the same way. Also, Islam is seen as a religion of peace and forgiveness is part of this.

A Muslims believe they should forgive criminals who do wrong.

B Forgiving others helps you to feel better.

C Muslims believe they should follow the example of Muhammad, who taught that forgiveness was important.

I would include point C because it offers a third reason (that is different to the **Suggested answer** first two) why forgiveness is important to Muslims.

I would not include point A because it states an idea about forgiveness rather **Suggested answer** than a belief about why it is important.

I would **not** include point B because Muslims do not believe forgiveness is a **Suggested answer** selfish action, so this idea does not answer the question asked.

42

Islam — Paper 2C Question 2

Reorder the answer

1 A student has written a plan to answer the question below. Decide which order the points should go in to structure a logical answer.

2 Explain **two** differences between Islamic beliefs about the afterlife and beliefs held by the main religious tradition of Great Britain. **(4 marks)**

Hints
There are two topics where you could be asked to compare and contrast beliefs between Islam and the main religious tradition of Great Britain (which is Christianity). The topics are 'Beliefs about the afterlife and their significance' and 'The practice and significance of worship'. The style of question is the same – you will need to state the similarities or differences (whichever you are asked for) and then add a second sentence to develop your answer.

1 Muslims believe angels have a role in their beliefs about the afterlife, whereas Christians do not.

4 Muslims emphasise that the person who has done wrong has to be sorry for their sins. Christians accept this same idea but also believe that the death of Jesus atoned for the sins of the world and repaired the relationship between God and humanity.

3 Muslims also believe that a person has to ask for forgiveness from God after death, whereas Christians believe that Jesus died for the sins of the whole world.

2 Islam teaches that throughout a person's life, angels record a person's good and bad actions then share these with Allah after death, for him to judge whether the person should go to paradise or to hell.

When a question asked me to compare or contrast different religions, I found it useful to create a quick list of similarities and differences before I answered the question.

2 A student has written a plan to answer the question below. Decide which order the points should go in to structure a logical answer.

2 Explain **two** similarities about why worship is important in Islam and to the followers of the main religious tradition of Great Britain. **(4 marks)**

1 Muslims and Christians both believe that worship is important to develop a relationship with God.

3 Muslims and Christians both believe that worship is important so they can ask God for help or support.

4 Both Muslims and Christians will pray when they want to ask God for forgiveness for something they have done wrong or for help if they are struggling in their lives.

2 They both pray regularly and have a holy day each week where they may attend a place of worship to worship with others of the same faith, so they can show commitment to God.

43

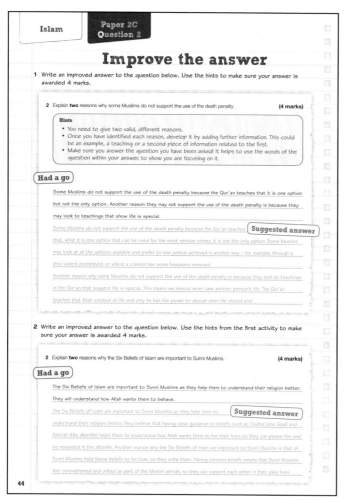

Islam — Paper 2C Question 2

Improve the answer

1 Write an improved answer to the question below. Use the hints to make sure your answer is awarded 4 marks.

2 Explain **two** reasons why some Muslims do not support the use of the death penalty. **(4 marks)**

Hints
- You need to give two valid, different reasons.
- Once you have identified each reason, develop it by adding further information. This could be an example, a teaching or a second piece of information related to the first.
- Make sure you answer the question you have been asked! It helps to use the words of the question within your answer, to show you are focusing on it.

Had a go

Some Muslims do not support the use of the death penalty because the Qur'an teaches that it is one option but not the only option. Another reason they may not support the use of the death penalty is because they may look to teachings that show life is special.

Suggested answer

Some Muslims do not support the use of the death penalty because the Qur'an teaches that, while it is one option that can be used for the most serious crimes, it is not the only option. Some Muslims may look at all the options available and prefer to see justice achieved in another way – for example, through a less violent punishment or where a criminal has some freedoms removed.

Another reason why some Muslims do not support the use of the death penalty is because they look to teachings in the Qur'an that suggest life is special. This means we should never take another person's life. The Qur'an teaches that Allah created all life and only he has the power to decide when life should end.

2 Write an improved answer to the question below. Use the hints from the first activity to make sure your answer is awarded 4 marks.

2 Explain **two** reasons why the Six Beliefs of Islam are important to Sunni Muslims. **(4 marks)**

Had a go

The Six Beliefs of Islam are important to Sunni Muslims as they help them to understand their religion better. They will understand how Allah wants them to behave.

Suggested answer

The Six Beliefs of Islam are important to Sunni Muslims as they help them to understand their religion better. They believe that having clear guidance on beliefs such as Tawhid (one God) and Akhirah (the afterlife) helps them to understand how Allah wants them to live their lives so they can please him and be rewarded in the afterlife. Another reason why the Six Beliefs of Islam are important to Sunni Muslims is that all Sunni Muslims hold these beliefs to be true, so they unite them. Having common beliefs means that Sunni Muslims feel strengthened and united as part of the Muslim ummah, so they can support each other in their daily lives.

44

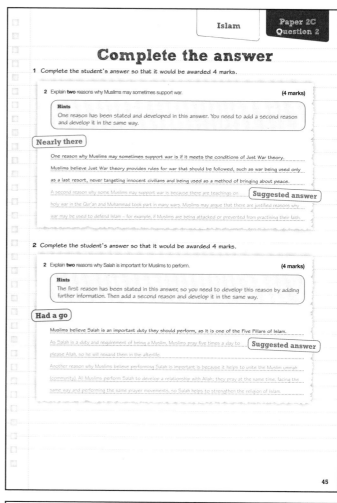

Islam — Paper 2C Question 2

Complete the answer

1 Complete the student's answer so that it would be awarded 4 marks.

2 Explain **two** reasons why Muslims may sometimes support war. **(4 marks)**

Hints
One reason has been stated and developed in this answer. You need to add a second reason and develop it in the same way.

Nearly there

One reason why Muslims may sometimes support war is if it meets the conditions of Just War theory. Muslims believe Just War theory provides rules for war that should be followed, such as war being used only as a last resort, never targeting innocent civilians and being used as a method of bringing about peace.

Suggested answer

A second reason why some Muslims may support war is because there are teachings on holy war in the Qur'an and Muhammad took part in many wars. Muslims may argue that there are justified reasons why war may be used to defend Islam – for example, if Muslims are being attacked or prevented from practising their faith.

2 Complete the student's answer so that it would be awarded 4 marks.

2 Explain **two** reasons why Salah is important for Muslims to perform. **(4 marks)**

Hints
The first reason has been stated in this answer, so you need to develop this reason by adding further information. Then add a second reason and develop it in the same way.

Had a go

Muslims believe Salah is an important duty they should perform, as it is one of the Five Pillars of Islam.

Suggested answer

As Salah is a duty and requirement of being a Muslim, Muslims pray five times a day to please Allah, so he will reward them in the afterlife.

Another reason why Muslims believe performing Salah is important is because it helps to unite the Muslim ummah (community). All Muslims perform Salah to develop a relationship with Allah; they pray at the same time, facing the same way and performing the same prayer movements, so Salah helps to strengthen the religion of Islam.

45

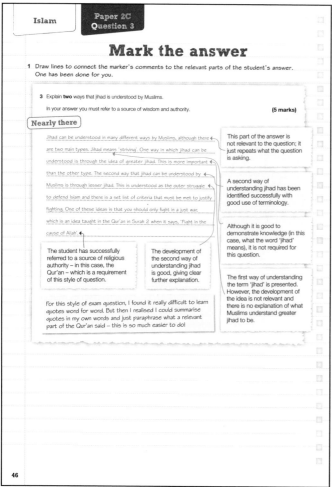

Islam — Paper 2C Question 3

Mark the answer

1 Draw lines to connect the marker's comments to the relevant parts of the student's answer. One has been done for you.

3 Explain **two** ways that jihad is understood by Muslims.

In your answer you must refer to a source of wisdom and authority. **(5 marks)**

Nearly there

Jihad can be understood in many different ways by Muslims, although there are two main types. Jihad means 'striving'. One way in which jihad can be understood is through the idea of greater jihad. This is more important than the other type. The second way that jihad can be understood by Muslims is through lesser jihad. This is understood as the outer struggle to defend Islam and there is a set list of criteria that must be met to justify fighting. One of these ideas is that you should only fight in a just war, which is an idea taught in the Qur'an in Surah 2 when it says, 'Fight in the cause of Allah.'

The student has successfully referred to a source of religious authority – in this case, the Qur'an – which is a requirement of this style of question.

The development of the second way of understanding jihad is good, giving clear further explanation.

This part of the answer is not relevant to the question; it just repeats what the question is asking.

A second way of understanding jihad has been identified successfully with good use of terminology.

Although it is good to demonstrate knowledge (in this case, what the word 'jihad' means), it is not required for this question.

The first way of understanding the term 'jihad' is presented. However, the development of the idea is not relevant and there is no explanation of what Muslims understand greater jihad to be.

For this style of exam question, I found it really difficult to learn quotes word for word. But then I realised I could summarise quotes in my own words and just paraphrase what a relevant part of the Qur'an said – this is so much easier to do!

46

Islam — Paper 2C Question 3

Mark the answer

1 Use the mark scheme below to decide how many marks you would award the student's answer in Activity 1 on the previous page.

When revising for the exams, it helped me to think about how my answer would be marked. I used this technique a lot to improve my confidence in how to answer exam questions.

Question	Answer
3 AO1 5 marks	Award one mark for each way and one mark for developing each way. Up to a maximum of four marks. Award one further mark for any relevant source of wisdom and authority. • Jihad can be understood as greater jihad. (1) This means that Muslims need to try to resist daily temptations in their lives and show commitment to Allah – for example, by praying five times a day, not drinking alcohol and studying the Qur'an. (1) The Qur'an teaches, 'establish prayer'. (1) • One way of understanding greater jihad is helping others. (1) The ummah (Muslim community) is seen as important in Islam and, through supporting others, it is understood as working for Allah. (1) Surah 9:71 teaches, 'The believing men and believing women are allies of each other'. (1) • Jihad can be understood through lesser jihad. (1) This is understood as fighting in the name of Allah. (1) The Qur'an teaches, 'Fight in the cause of Allah those who fight you'. (1)

There may be other valid answers, but for this activity use the mark scheme given.

Suggested answer

I would award the answer **4** marks because it states two valid ways of understanding the term 'jihad'. The first idea is not developed, so it would achieve only 1 mark. The second idea is stated and developed, so it would achieve 2 marks. The second idea also has a relevant reference to a source of wisdom and authority, which achieves another 1 mark.

Suggested answer

The improvements I would make to this answer are to remove the first irrelevant part of the answer; develop the first way of understanding greater jihad, and put the quote into my own words.

47

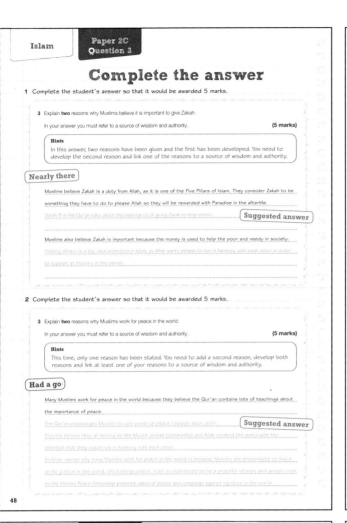

Complete the answer

1 Complete the student's answer so that it would be awarded 5 marks.

> 3 Explain **two** reasons why Muslims believe it is important to give Zakah.
>
> In your answer you must refer to a source of wisdom and authority. **(5 marks)**
>
> **Hints**
> In this answer, two reasons have been given and the first has been developed. You need to develop the second reason and link one of the reasons to a source of wisdom and authority.

Nearly there

Muslims believe Zakah is a duty from Allah, as it is one of the Five Pillars of Islam. They consider Zakah to be something they have to do to please Allah so they will be rewarded with Paradise in the afterlife.

Surah 9 in the Qur'an talks about the importance of giving Zakah to help others. ____ **Suggested answer**

Muslims also believe Zakah is important because the money is used to help the poor and needy in society.

Helping others is a key idea promoted in Islam, as Allah wants people to live in harmony with each other in order to support all Muslims in the ummah.

2 Complete the student's answer so that it would be awarded 5 marks.

> 3 Explain **two** reasons why Muslims work for peace in the world.
>
> In your answer you must refer to a source of wisdom and authority. **(5 marks)**
>
> **Hints**
> This time, only one reason has been stated. You need to add a second reason, develop both reasons and link at least one of your reasons to a source of wisdom and authority.

Had a go

Many Muslims work for peace in the world because they believe the Qur'an contains lots of teachings about the importance of peace.

The Qur'an encourages Muslims to use words of peace towards each other. ____ **Suggested answer**

Muslims believe they all belong to the Muslim ummah (community) and Allah created the world with the intention that they would live in harmony with each other.

Another reason why many Muslims work for peace in the world is because Muslims are encouraged to stand up for justice in the world, which brings peace. Islam is understood to be a peaceful religion, and groups such as the Muslim Peace Fellowship promote ideas of peace and campaign against injustice in the world.

48

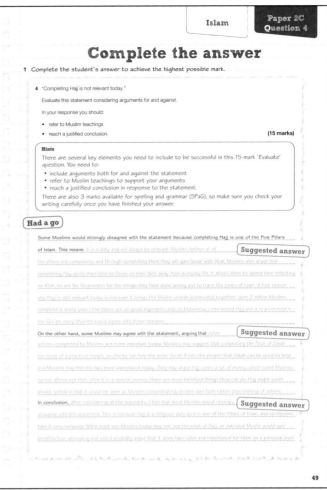

Complete the answer

1 Complete the student's answer to achieve the highest possible mark.

> 4 "Completing Hajj is not relevant today."
>
> Evaluate this statement considering arguments for and against.
>
> In your response you should:
> - refer to Muslim teachings
> - reach a justified conclusion. **(15 marks)**
>
> **Hints**
> There are several key elements you need to include to be successful in this 15-mark 'Evaluate' question. You need to:
> - include arguments both for and against the statement
> - refer to Muslim teachings to support your arguments
> - reach a justified conclusion in response to the statement.
> There are also 3 marks available for spelling and grammar (SPaG), so make sure you check your writing carefully once you have finished your answer.

Had a go

Some Muslims would strongly disagree with the statement because completing Hajj is one of the Five Pillars of Islam. This means it is a duty and will always be relevant. Muslims believe all of ____ **Suggested answer**
the pillars are compulsory and through completing them they will gain favour with Allah. Muslims also argue that completing Hajj gives them time to focus on their faith away from everyday life. It allows them to spend time reflecting on Allah, to ask for forgiveness for the things they have done wrong and to trace the roots of Islam. A final reason why Hajj is still relevant today is because it brings the Muslim ummah (community) together: over 2 million Muslims complete it every year. I feel these are all good arguments and, as Muhammad commanded Hajj and it is promoted in the Qur'an, many Muslims would agree with these reasons.

On the other hand, some Muslims may agree with the statement, arguing that other ____ **Suggested answer**
actions completed by Muslims are more important today. Muslims may suggest that completing the Pillar of Zakah has more of a practical impact, as charity can help the poor (Surah 9 lists the people that Zakah can be used to help), and Muslims may feel this has more importance today. They may argue Hajj costs a lot of money, which some Muslims cannot afford and that, while it is a special journey, there are more beneficial things they can do. Hajj might seem almost selfish in that it could be seen as Muslims concentrating on their own faith rather than thinking of others.

In conclusion, after considering all the arguments, I feel that most Muslims would strongly ____ **Suggested answer**
disagree with the statement. This is because Hajj is a religious duty as it is one of the Pillars of Islam, and so Muslims take it very seriously. While most non-Muslims today may not see the point of Hajj, an individual Muslim would gain benefits from attending and would probably argue that it does have value and importance for them on a personal level.

49

Reorder the answer

1 A student has written a plan to answer this question. Decide which of their points support the statement and which counter it. Mark each with an S (support) or C (counter). One has been done for you.

> 4 "The most important aim of punishment is for the criminal to reform."
>
> Evaluate this statement considering arguments for and against.
>
> In your response you should:
> - refer to Muslim teachings
> - refer to different Muslim points of view
> - reach a justified conclusion. **(12 marks)**
>
> **Hints**
> Always read the bullets in the 'Evaluate' questions carefully. Sometimes they only ask for teachings, but sometimes you have to include differing Muslim views or reference to ethical theories.
> You should also check whether there are 3 marks available for SPaG for this type of question. If there are, an instruction will be given in bold above the exam question, and the question will be worth 15 marks instead of 12.

Had a go

C	Protecting society from dangerous criminals is seen to be important, as all human life is created by Allah and is therefore sacred. Imprisoning criminals means society is safe.
S	Islam teaches that it is important for criminals to be given the opportunity to understand why their behaviour was wrong and to change through being sorry for what they have done. Islam teaches the importance of forgiveness, so that everyone involved can move on.
S	While the punishment of criminals is accepted as necessary, many Muslims look to teachings that suggest people need help to change. Muslim organisations such as the Muslim Chaplains' Association or Mosaic can provide support with the rehabilitation of offenders so they understand why their actions were wrong and do not reoffend.
S	Islam teaches that Allah is forgiving and gives humans a second chance, so many Muslims believe Allah wants humans to behave in a similar way towards each other. Forgiveness is part of allowing a criminal to change their behaviour.
S	Surah 4:26–28 teaches the importance of people accepting that what they have done is wrong and trying to change their behaviour.
C	Justice is important to Muslims, and one aim of punishment is upholding the law and making sure everyone sees that justice is achieved. Punishments may also deter others from turning to crime.

Lots of the topics studied are controversial and different Muslims have different views. Before I start writing my response, I find it useful to plan my answer by considering these different views and then identifying the reasons for each view.

50

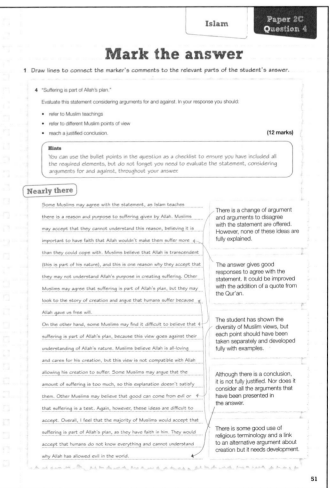

Mark the answer

1 Draw lines to connect the marker's comments to the relevant parts of the student's answer.

> 4 "Suffering is part of Allah's plan."
>
> Evaluate this statement considering arguments for and against. In your response you should:
> - refer to Muslim teachings
> - refer to different Muslim points of view
> - reach a justified conclusion. **(12 marks)**
>
> **Hints**
> You can use the bullet points in the question as a checklist to ensure you have included all the required elements, but do not forget you need to evaluate the statement, considering arguments for and against, throughout your answer.

Nearly there

Some Muslims may agree with the statement, as Islam teaches there is a reason and purpose to suffering given by Allah. Muslims may accept that they cannot understand this reason, believing it is important to have faith that Allah wouldn't make them suffer more than they could cope with. Muslims believe that Allah is transcendent (this is part of his nature), and this is one reason why they accept that they may not understand Allah's purpose in creating suffering. Other Muslims may agree that suffering is part of Allah's plan, but they may look to the story of creation and argue that humans suffer because Allah gave us free will.

On the other hand, some Muslims may find it difficult to believe that suffering is part of Allah's plan, because this view goes against their understanding of Allah's nature. Muslims believe Allah is all-loving and cares for his creation, but this view is not compatible with Allah allowing his creation to suffer. Some Muslims may argue that the amount of suffering is too much, so this explanation doesn't satisfy them. Other Muslims may believe that good can come from evil or that suffering is a test. Again, however, these ideas are difficult to accept. Overall, I feel that the majority of Muslims would accept that suffering is part of Allah's plan, as they have faith in him. They would accept that humans do not know everything and cannot understand why Allah has allowed evil in the world.

Marker's comments:
- There is a change of argument and arguments to disagree with the statement are offered. However, none of these ideas are fully explained.
- The answer gives good responses to agree with the statement. It could be improved with the addition of a quote from the Qur'an.
- The student has shown the diversity of Muslim views, but each point should have been taken separately and developed fully with examples.
- Although there is a conclusion, it is not fully justified. Nor does it consider all the arguments that have been presented in the answer.
- There is some good use of religious terminology and a link to an alternative argument about creation but it needs development.

51

Answers

Mark the answer

1 Use the mark scheme to decide to which of these answers you would **not** award full marks. Explain your choice.

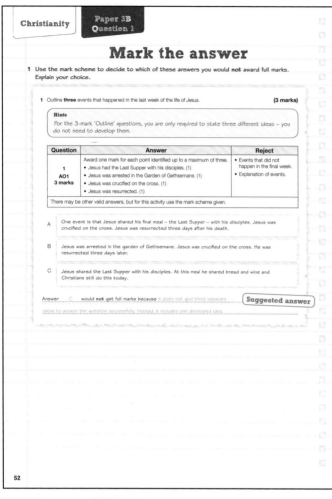

1 Outline **three** events that happened in the last week of the life of Jesus. **(3 marks)**

Hints
For the 3-mark 'Outline' questions, you are only required to state three different ideas – you do not need to develop them.

Question	Answer	Reject
1 AO1 3 marks	Award one mark for each point identified up to a maximum of three. • Jesus had the Last Supper with his disciples. (1) • Jesus was arrested in the Garden of Gethsemane. (1) • Jesus was crucified on the cross. (1) • Jesus was resurrected. (1)	• Events that did not happen in the final week. • Explanation of events.

There may be other valid answers, but for this activity use the mark scheme given.

A One event is that Jesus shared his final meal – the Last Supper – with his disciples. Jesus was crucified on the cross. Jesus was resurrected three days after his death.

B Jesus was arrested in the garden of Gethsemane. Jesus was crucified on the cross. He was resurrected three days later.

C Jesus shared the Last Supper with his disciples. At this meal he shared bread and wine and Christians still do this today.

Answer ___C___ would **not** get full marks because it does not give three separate ideas to answer the question successfully. Instead, it includes one developed idea. **Suggested answer**

52

Complete the question

1 Use the student's answer to complete the question.

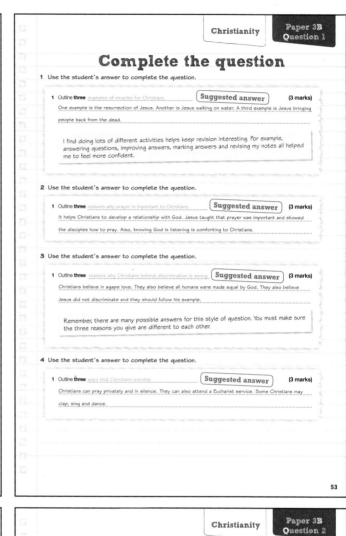

1 Outline **three** examples of miracles for Christians. **Suggested answer** **(3 marks)**
One example is the resurrection of Jesus. Another is Jesus walking on water. A third example is Jesus bringing people back from the dead.

I find doing lots of different activities helps keep revision interesting. For example, answering questions, improving answers, marking answers and revising my notes all helped me to feel more confident.

2 Use the student's answer to complete the question.

1 Outline **three** reasons why prayer is important to Christians. **Suggested answer** **(3 marks)**
It helps Christians to develop a relationship with God. Jesus taught that prayer was important and showed the disciples how to pray. Also, knowing God is listening is comforting to Christians.

3 Use the student's answer to complete the question.

1 Outline **three** reasons why Christians believe discrimination is wrong. **Suggested answer** **(3 marks)**
Christians believe in agape love. They also believe all humans were made equal by God. They also believe Jesus did not discriminate and they should follow his example.

Remember, there are many possible answers for this style of question. You must make sure the three reasons you give are different to each other.

4 Use the student's answer to complete the question.

1 Outline **three** ways that Christians worship. **Suggested answer** **(3 marks)**
Christians can pray privately and in silence. They can also attend a Eucharist service. Some Christians may clap, sing and dance.

53

Complete the answer

1 Complete the student's answer so that it would be awarded 3 marks.

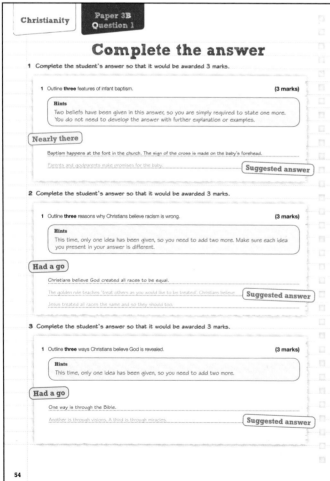

1 Outline **three** features of infant baptism. **(3 marks)**

Hints
Two beliefs have been given in this answer, so you are simply required to state one more. You do not need to develop the answer with further explanation or examples.

Nearly there
Baptism happens at the font in the church. The sign of the cross is made on the baby's forehead.
Parents and godparents make promises for the baby. **Suggested answer**

2 Complete the student's answer so that it would be awarded 3 marks.

1 Outline **three** reasons why Christians believe racism is wrong. **(3 marks)**

Hints
This time, only one idea has been given, so you need to add two more. Make sure each idea you present in your answer is different.

Had a go
Christians believe God created all races to be equal.
The golden rule teaches 'treat others as you would like to be treated'. Christians believe **Suggested answer**
Jesus treated all races the same and so they should too.

3 Complete the student's answer so that it would be awarded 3 marks.

1 Outline **three** ways Christians believe God is revealed. **(3 marks)**

Hints
This time, only one idea has been given, so you need to add two more.

Had a go
One way is through the Bible.
Another is through visions. A third is through miracles. **Suggested answer**

54

Mark the answer

1 Draw lines to connect the marker's comments to the relevant parts of the student's answer. One has been done for you.

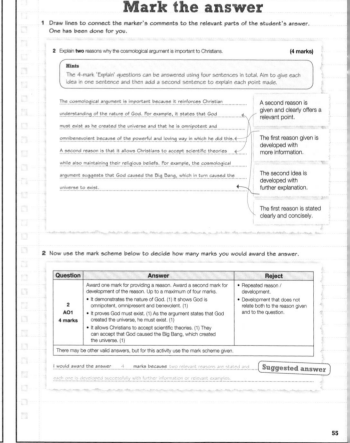

2 Explain **two** reasons why the cosmological argument is important to Christians. **(4 marks)**

Hints
The 4-mark 'Explain' questions can be answered using four sentences in total. Aim to give each idea in one sentence and then add a second sentence to explain each point made.

The cosmological argument is important because it reinforces Christian understanding of the nature of God. For example, it states that God must exist as he created the universe and that he is omnipotent and omnibenevolent because of the powerful and loving way in which he did this. A second reason is that it allows Christians to accept scientific theories while also maintaining their religious beliefs. For example, the cosmological argument suggests that God caused the Big Bang, which in turn caused the universe to exist.

- A second reason is given and clearly offers a relevant point.
- The first reason given is developed with more information.
- The second idea is developed with further explanation.
- The first reason is stated clearly and concisely.

2 Now use the mark scheme below to decide how many marks you would award the answer.

Question	Answer	Reject
2 AO1 4 marks	Award one mark for providing a reason. Award a second mark for development of the reason. Up to a maximum of four marks. • It demonstrates the nature of God. (1) It shows God is omnipotent, omnipresent and benevolent. (1) • It proves God must exist. (1) As the argument states that God created the universe, he must exist. (1) • It allows Christians to accept scientific theories. (1) They can accept that God caused the Big Bang, which created the universe. (1)	• Repeated reason / development. • Development that does not relate both to the reason given and to the question.

There may be other valid answers, but for this activity use the mark scheme given.

I would award the answer ___4___ marks because two relevant reasons are stated and each one is developed successfully with further information or relevant examples. **Suggested answer**

55

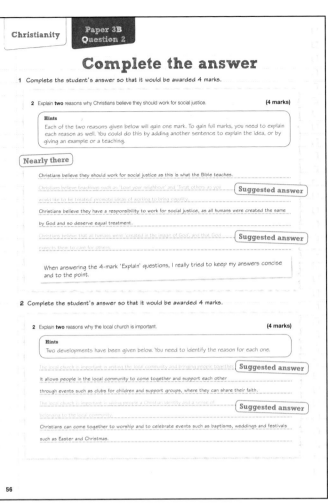

Christianity — Paper 3B Question 2

Complete the answer

1 Complete the student's answer so that it would be awarded 4 marks.

2 Explain **two** reasons why Christians believe they should work for social justice. (4 marks)

Hints
Each of the two reasons given below will gain one mark. To gain full marks, you need to explain each reason as well. You could do this by adding another sentence to explain the idea, or by giving an example or a teaching.

Nearly there

Christians believe they should work for social justice as this is what the Bible teaches.

Christians believe teachings such as 'Love your neighbour' and 'Treat others as you [**Suggested answer**]
would like to be treated' promote ideas of working to bring equality.

Christians believe they have a responsibility to work for social justice, as all humans were created the same by God and so deserve equal treatment.

Christians believe that all humans were 'created in the image of God', and that God [**Suggested answer**]
came to them to care for others.

When answering the 4-mark 'Explain' questions, I really tried to keep my answers concise and to the point.

2 Complete the student's answer so that it would be awarded 4 marks.

2 Explain **two** reasons why the local church is important. (4 marks)

Hints
Two developments have been given below. You need to identify the reason for each one.

The local church is important in uniting the local community and bringing people together. [**Suggested answer**]
It allows people in the local community to come together and support each other through events such as clubs for children and support groups, where they can share their faith.

The local church is important in giving people a Christian identity and a sense of [**Suggested answer**]
belonging to the local community.
Christians can come together to worship and to celebrate events such as baptisms, weddings and festivals such as Easter and Christmas.

56

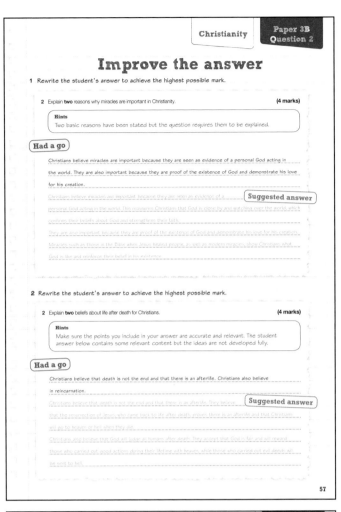

Christianity — Paper 3B Question 2

Improve the answer

1 Rewrite the student's answer to achieve the highest possible mark.

2 Explain **two** reasons why miracles are important in Christianity. (4 marks)

Hints
Two basic reasons have been stated but the question requires them to be explained.

Had a go

Christians believe miracles are important because they are seen as evidence of a personal God acting in the world. They are also important because they are proof of the existence of God and demonstrate his love for his creation.

Christians believe miracles are important because they are seen as evidence of a [**Suggested answer**]
personal God acting in the world. This reassures Christians that God is close by and watching over the world, which confirms their beliefs about God and strengthens their faith.

They are also important because they are proof of the existence of God and demonstrate his love for his creation. Miracles such as those in the Bible when Jesus healed people, as well as modern miracles, show Christians what God is like and reinforce their belief in his existence.

2 Rewrite the student's answer to achieve the highest possible mark.

2 Explain **two** beliefs about life after death for Christians. (4 marks)

Hints
Make sure the points you include in your answer are accurate and relevant. The student answer below contains some relevant content but the ideas are not developed fully.

Had a go

Christians believe that death is not the end and that there is an afterlife. Christians also believe in reincarnation.

Christians believe that death is not the end and that there is an afterlife. They believe [**Suggested answer**]
that the resurrection of Jesus, who came back to life after death, proves there is an afterlife and that Christians will go to heaven or hell when they die.

Christians also believe that God will judge all humans after death. They accept that God is fair and will reward those who carried out good actions during their lifetime with heaven, while those who carried out evil deeds will be sent to hell.

57

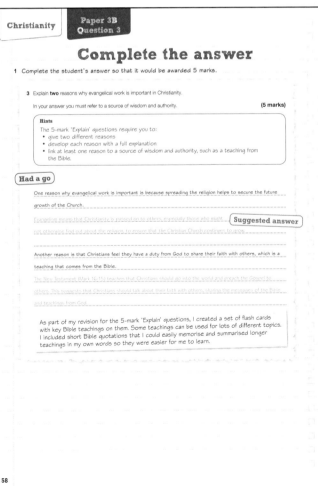

Christianity — Paper 3B Question 3

Complete the answer

1 Complete the student's answer so that it would be awarded 5 marks.

3 Explain **two** reasons why evangelical work is important in Christianity.
In your answer you must refer to a source of wisdom and authority. (5 marks)

Hints
The 5-mark 'Explain' questions require you to:
• give two different reasons
• develop each reason with a full explanation
• link at least one reason to a source of wisdom and authority, such as a teaching from the Bible.

Had a go

One reason why evangelical work is important is because spreading the religion helps to secure the future growth of the Church.

Evangelism means that Christianity is passed on to others, especially those who might [**Suggested answer**]
not otherwise find out about the religion, to ensure that the Christian Church continues to grow.

Another reason is that Christians feel they have a duty from God to share their faith with others, which is a teaching that comes from the Bible.

The New Testament (Mark 16:15) teaches that Christians should go into the world and preach the Gospel to others. This suggests that Christians should talk about their faith with others, sharing the message of the Bible and teachings from God.

As part of my revision for the 5-mark 'Explain' questions, I created a set of flash cards with key Bible teachings on them. Some teachings can be used for lots of different topics. I included short Bible quotations that I could easily memorise and summarised longer teachings in my own words so they were easier for me to learn.

58

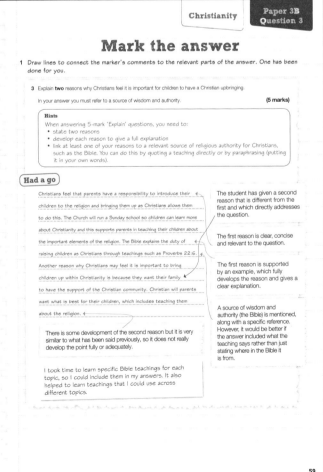

Christianity — Paper 3B Question 3

Mark the answer

1 Draw lines to connect the marker's comments to the relevant parts of the answer. One has been done for you.

3 Explain **two** reasons why Christians feel it is important for children to have a Christian upbringing.
In your answer you must refer to a source of wisdom and authority. (5 marks)

Hints
When answering 5-mark 'Explain' questions, you need to:
• state two reasons
• develop each reason to give a full explanation
• link at least one of your reasons to a relevant source of religious authority for Christians, such as the Bible. You can do this by quoting a teaching directly or by paraphrasing (putting it in your own words).

Had a go

Christians feel that parents have a responsibility to introduce their children to the religion and bringing them up as Christians allows them to do this. The Church will run a Sunday school so children can learn more about Christianity and this supports parents in teaching their children about the important elements of the religion. The Bible explains the duty of raising children as Christians through teachings such as Proverbs 22:6.

Another reason why Christians may feel it is important to bring children up within Christianity is because they want their family to have the support of the Christian community. Christian will parents want what is best for their children, which includes teaching them about the religion.

The student has given a second reason that is different from the first and which directly addresses the question.

The first reason is clear, concise and relevant to the question.

The first reason is supported by an example, which fully develops the reason and gives a clear explanation.

A source of wisdom and authority (the Bible) is mentioned, along with a specific reference. However, it would be better if the answer included what the teaching says rather than just stating where in the Bible it is from.

There is some development of the second reason but it is very similar to what has been said previously, so it does not really develop the point fully or adequately.

I took time to learn specific Bible teachings for each topic, so I could include them in my answers. It also helped to learn teachings that I could use across different topics.

59

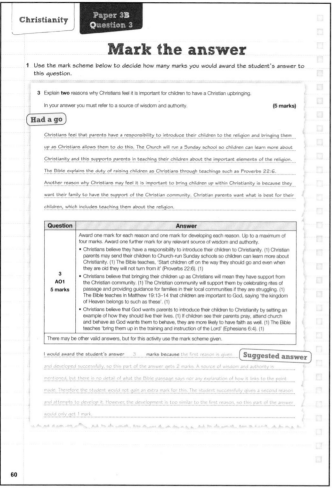

Christianity | Paper 3B Question 3

Mark the answer

1 Use the mark scheme below to decide how many marks you would award the student's answer to this question.

3 Explain **two** reasons why Christians feel it is important for children to have a Christian upbringing.

In your answer you must refer to a source of wisdom and authority. **(5 marks)**

Had a go

Christians feel that parents have a responsibility to introduce their children to the religion and bringing them up as Christians allows them to do this. The Church will run a Sunday school so children can learn more about Christianity and this supports parents in teaching their children about the important elements of the religion. The Bible explains the duty of raising children as Christians through teachings such as Proverbs 22:6. Another reason why Christians may feel it is important to bring children up within Christianity is because they want their family to have the support of the Christian community. Christian parents want what is best for their children, which includes teaching them about the religion.

Question	Answer
3 AO1 5 marks	Award one mark for each reason and one mark for developing each reason. Up to a maximum of four marks. Award one further mark for any relevant source of wisdom and authority. • Christians believe they have a responsibility to introduce their children to Christianity. (1) Christian parents may send their children to Church-run Sunday schools so children can learn more about Christianity. (1) The Bible teaches, 'Start children off on the way they should go and even when they are old they will not turn from it' (Proverbs 22:6). (1) • Christians believe that bringing their children up as Christians will mean they have support from the Christian community. (1) The Christian community will support them by celebrating rites of passage and providing guidance for families in their local communities if they are struggling. (1) The Bible teaches in Matthew 19:13–14 that children are important to God, saying 'the kingdom of Heaven belongs to such as these'. (1) • Christians believe that God wants parents to introduce their children to Christianity by setting an example of how they should live their lives. (1) If children see their parents pray, attend church and behave as God wants them to behave, they are more likely to have faith as well. (1) The Bible teaches 'bring them up in the training and instruction of the Lord' (Ephesians 6:4). (1)
There may be other valid answers, but for this activity use the mark scheme given.	

Suggested answer

I would award the student's answer 3 marks because the first reason is given and developed successfully, so this part of the answer gets 2 marks. A source of wisdom and authority is mentioned, but there is no detail of what the Bible passage says nor any explanation of how it links to the point made. Therefore the student would not gain an extra mark for this. The student successfully gives a second reason and attempts to develop it. However, the development is too similar to the first reason, so this part of the answer would only get 1 mark.

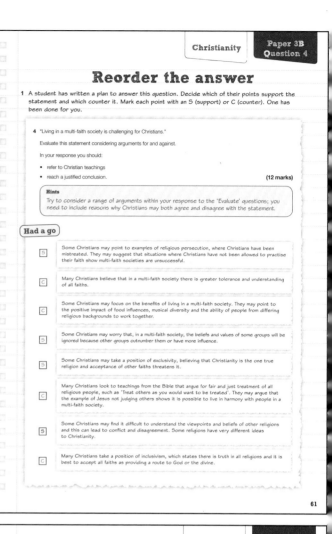

60

Christianity | Paper 3B Question 4

Reorder the answer

1 A student has written a plan to answer this question. Decide which of their points support the statement and which counter it. Mark each point with an S (support) or C (counter). One has been done for you.

4 "Living in a multi-faith society is challenging for Christians."

Evaluate this statement considering arguments for and against.

In your response you should:

- refer to Christian teachings
- reach a justified conclusion. **(12 marks)**

Hints
Try to consider a range of arguments within your response to the 'Evaluate' questions; you need to include reasons why Christians may both agree and disagree with the statement.

Had a go

S	Some Christians may point to examples of religious persecution, where Christians have been mistreated. They may suggest that situations where Christians have not been allowed to practise their faith show multi-faith societies are unsuccessful.
C	Many Christians believe that in a multi-faith society there is greater tolerance and understanding of all faiths.
C	Some Christians may focus on the benefits of living in a multi-faith society. They may point to the positive impact of food influences, musical diversity and the ability of people from differing religious backgrounds to work together.
S	Some Christians may worry that, in a multi-faith society, the beliefs and values of some groups will be ignored because other groups outnumber them or have more influence.
S	Some Christians may take a position of exclusivity, believing that Christianity is the one true religion and acceptance of other faiths threatens it.
C	Many Christians look to teachings from the Bible that argue for fair and just treatment of all religious people, such as 'Treat others as you would want to be treated'. They may argue that the example of Jesus not judging others shows it is possible to live in harmony with people in a multi-faith society.
S	Some Christians may find it difficult to understand the viewpoints and beliefs of other religions and this can lead to conflict and disagreement. Some religions have very different ideas to Christianity.
C	Many Christians take a position of inclusivism, which states there is truth in all religions and it is best to accept all faiths as providing a route to God or the divine.

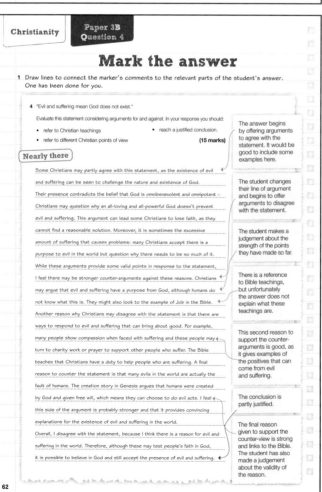

61

Christianity | Paper 3B Question 4

Mark the answer

1 Draw lines to connect the marker's comments to the relevant parts of the student's answer. One has been done for you.

4 "Evil and suffering mean God does not exist."

Evaluate this statement considering arguments for and against. In your response you should:

- refer to Christian teachings
- refer to different Christian points of view
- reach a justified conclusion. **(15 marks)**

Nearly there

Some Christians may partly agree with this statement, as the existence of evil and suffering can be seen to challenge the nature and existence of God. Their presence contradicts the belief that God is omnibenevolent and omnipotent – Christians may question why an all-loving and all-powerful God doesn't prevent evil and suffering. This argument can lead some Christians to lose faith, as they cannot find a reasonable solution. Moreover, it is sometimes the excessive amount of suffering that causes problems: many Christians accept there is a purpose to evil in the world but question why there needs to be so much of it. While these arguments provide some valid points in response to the statement, I feel there may be stronger counter-arguments against these reasons. Christians may argue that evil and suffering have a purpose from God, although humans do not know what this is. They might also look to the example of Job in the Bible. Another reason why Christians may disagree with the statement is that there are ways to respond to evil and suffering that can bring about good. For example, many people show compassion when faced with suffering and these people may turn to charity work or prayer to support other people who suffer. The Bible teaches that Christians have a duty to help people who are suffering. A final reason to counter the statement is that many evils in the world are actually the fault of humans. The creation story in Genesis argues that humans were created by God and given free will, which means they can choose to do evil acts. I feel this side of the argument is probably stronger and that it provides convincing explanations for the existence of evil and suffering in the world. Overall, I disagree with the statement, because I think there is a reason for evil and suffering in the world. Therefore, although these may test people's faith in God, it is possible to believe in God and still accept the presence of evil and suffering.

The answer begins by offering arguments to agree with the statement. It would be good to include some examples here.

The student changes their line of argument and begins to offer arguments to disagree with the statement.

The student makes a judgement about the strength of the points they have made so far.

There is a reference to Bible teachings, but unfortunately the answer does not explain what these teachings are.

This second reason to support the counter-arguments is good, as it gives examples of the positives that can come from evil and suffering.

The conclusion is partly justified.

The final reason given to support the counter-view is strong and links to the Bible. The student has also made a judgement about the validity of the reason.

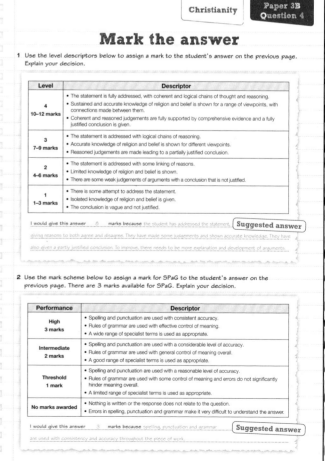

62

Christianity | Paper 3B Question 4

Mark the answer

1 Use the level descriptors below to assign a mark to the student's answer on the previous page. Explain your decision.

Level	Descriptor
4 10–12 marks	• The statement is fully addressed, with coherent and logical chains of thought and reasoning. • Sustained and accurate knowledge of religion and belief is shown for a range of viewpoints, with connections made between them. • Coherent and reasoned judgements are fully supported by comprehensive evidence and a fully justified conclusion is given.
3 7–9 marks	• The statement is addressed with logical chains of reasoning. • Accurate knowledge of religion and belief is shown for different viewpoints. • Reasoned judgements are made leading to a partially justified conclusion.
2 4–6 marks	• The statement is addressed with some linking of reasons. • Limited knowledge of religion and belief is shown. • There are some weak judgements of arguments with a conclusion that is not justified.
1 1–3 marks	• There is some attempt to address the statement. • Isolated knowledge of religion and belief is given. • The conclusion is vague and not justified.

Suggested answer

I would give this answer 8 marks because the student has addressed the statement, giving reasons to both agree and disagree. They have made some judgements and shown accurate knowledge. They have also given a partly justified conclusion. To improve, there needs to be more explanation and development of arguments.

2 Use the mark scheme below to assign a mark for SPaG to the student's answer on the previous page. There are 3 marks available for SPaG. Explain your decision.

Performance	Descriptor
High 3 marks	• Spelling and punctuation are used with consistent accuracy. • Rules of grammar are used with effective control of meaning. • A wide range of specialist terms is used as appropriate.
Intermediate 2 marks	• Spelling and punctuation are used with a considerable level of accuracy. • Rules of grammar are used with general control of meaning overall. • A good range of specialist terms is used as appropriate.
Threshold 1 mark	• Spelling and punctuation are used with a reasonable level of accuracy. • Rules of grammar are used with some control of meaning and errors do not significantly hinder meaning overall. • A limited range of specialist terms is used as appropriate.
No marks awarded	• Nothing is written or the response does not relate to the question. • Errors in spelling, punctuation and grammar make it very difficult to understand the answer.

Suggested answer

I would give this answer 3 marks because spelling, punctuation and grammar are used with consistency and accuracy throughout the piece of work.

63

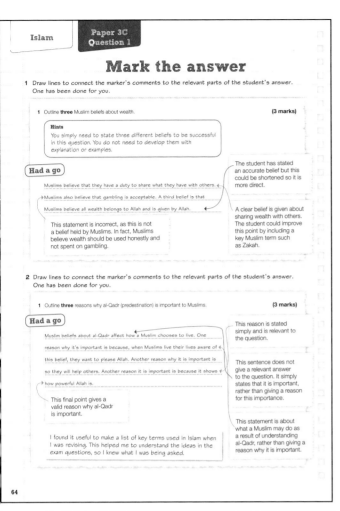

Islam — Paper 3C Question 1

Mark the answer

1 Draw lines to connect the marker's comments to the relevant parts of the student's answer. One has been done for you.

1 Outline **three** Muslim beliefs about wealth. (3 marks)

Hints
You simply need to state three different beliefs to be successful in this question. You do not need to develop them with explanation or examples.

Had a go

Muslims believe that they have a duty to share what they have with others.

Muslims also believe that gambling is acceptable. A third belief is that Muslims believe all wealth belongs to Allah and is given by Allah.

The student has stated an accurate belief but this could be shortened so it is more direct.

A clear belief is given about sharing wealth with others. The student could improve this point by including a key Muslim term such as Zakah.

This statement is incorrect, as this is not a belief held by Muslims. In fact, Muslims believe wealth should be used honestly and not spent on gambling.

2 Draw lines to connect the marker's comments to the relevant parts of the student's answer. One has been done for you.

1 Outline **three** reasons why al-Qadr (predestination) is important to Muslims. (3 marks)

Had a go

Muslim beliefs about al-Qadr affect how a Muslim chooses to live. One reason why it's important is because, when Muslims live their lives aware of this belief, they want to please Allah. Another reason why it is important is so they will help others. Another reason it is important is because it shows how powerful Allah is.

This reason is stated simply and is relevant to the question.

This sentence does not give a relevant answer to the question. It simply states that it is important, rather than giving a reason for this importance.

This final point gives a valid reason why al-Qadr is important.

This statement is about what a Muslim may do as a result of understanding al-Qadr, rather than giving a reason why it is important.

I found it useful to make a list of key terms used in Islam when I was revising. This helped me to understand the ideas in the exam questions, so I knew what I was being asked.

64

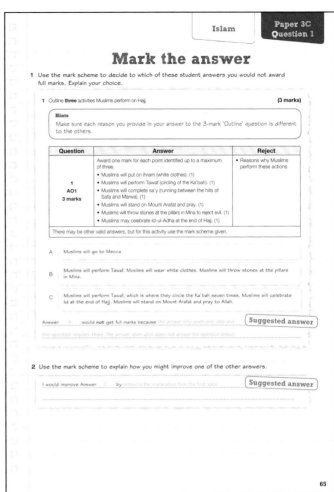

Islam — Paper 3C Question 1

Mark the answer

1 Use the mark scheme to decide to which of these student answers you would not award full marks. Explain your choice.

1 Outline **three** activities Muslims perform on Hajj. (3 marks)

Hints
Make sure each reason you provide in your answer to the 3-mark 'Outline' question is different to the others.

Question	Answer	Reject
1 AO1 3 marks	Award one mark for each point identified up to a maximum of three. • Muslims will put on ihram (white clothes). (1) • Muslims will perform Tawaf (circling of the Ka'bah). (1) • Muslims will complete sa'y (running between the hills of Safa and Marwa). (1) • Muslims will stand on Mount Arafat and pray. (1) • Muslims will throw stones at the pillars in Mina to reject evil. (1) • Muslims may celebrate Id-ul-Adha at the end of Hajj. (1)	• Reasons why Muslims perform these actions.

There may be other valid answers, but for this activity use the mark scheme given.

A Muslims will go to Mecca.

B Muslims will perform Tawaf. Muslims will wear white clothes. Muslims will throw stones at the pillars in Mina.

C Muslims will perform Tawaf, which is where they circle the Ka'bah seven times. Muslims will celebrate Id at the end of Hajj. Muslims will stand on Mount Arafat and pray to Allah.

Answer A would **not** get full marks because the answer only gives one idea and this question requires three. The answer given also does not answer the question asked. [Suggested answer]

2 Use the mark scheme to explain how you might improve one of the other answers.

I would improve Answer C by removing the explanation from the first idea. [Suggested answer]

65

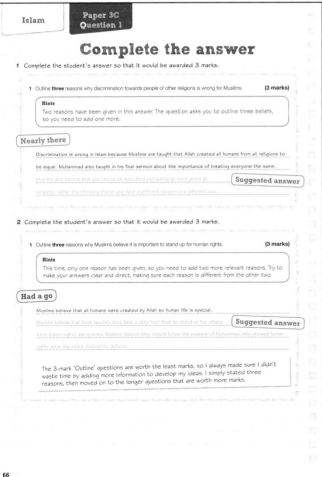

Islam — Paper 3C Question 1

Complete the answer

1 Complete the student's answer so that it would be awarded 3 marks.

1 Outline **three** reasons why discrimination towards people of other religions is wrong for Muslims. (3 marks)

Hints
Two reasons have been given in this answer. The question asks you to outline three beliefs, so you need to add one more.

Nearly there

Discrimination is wrong in Islam because Muslims are taught that Allah created all humans from all religions to be equal. Muhammad also taught in his final sermon about the importance of treating everyone the same. Muslims also believe that you should be educated and willing to learn about all religions, rather than treating those who have a different religion in a different way. [Suggested answer]

2 Complete the student's answer so that it would be awarded 3 marks.

1 Outline **three** reasons why Muslims believe it is important to stand up for human rights. (3 marks)

Hints
This time, only one reason has been given, so you need to add two more relevant reasons. Try to make your answers clear and direct, making sure each reason is different from the other two.

Had a go

Muslims believe that all humans were created by Allah so human life is special. Muslims believe that Islam teaches they have a duty from Allah to stand up for others when human rights are ignored. Muslims believe they should follow the example of Muhammad, who showed human rights were important through his actions. [Suggested answer]

The 3-mark 'Outline' questions are worth the least marks, so I always made sure I didn't waste time by adding more information to develop my ideas. I simply stated three reasons, then moved on to the longer questions that are worth more marks.

66

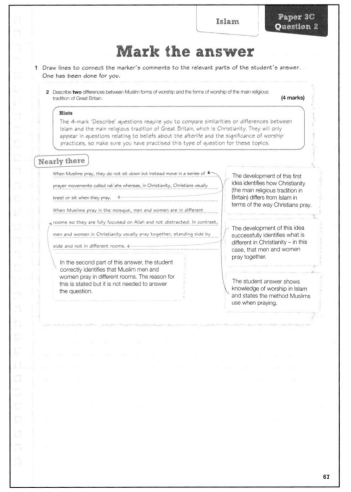

Islam — Paper 3C Question 2

Mark the answer

1 Draw lines to connect the marker's comments to the relevant parts of the student's answer. One has been done for you.

2 Describe **two** differences between Muslim forms of worship and the forms of worship of the main religious tradition of Great Britain. (4 marks)

Hints
The 4-mark 'Describe' questions require you to compare similarities or differences between Islam and the main religious tradition of Great Britain, which is Christianity. They will only appear in questions relating to beliefs about the afterlife and the significance of worship practices, so make sure you have practised this type of question for these topics.

Nearly there

When Muslims pray, they do not sit down but instead move in a series of prayer movements called rak'ahs whereas, in Christianity, Christians usually kneel or sit when they pray.

When Muslims pray in the mosque, men and women are in different rooms so they are fully focused on Allah and not distracted. In contrast, men and women in Christianity usually pray together, standing side by side and not in different rooms.

The development of this first idea identifies how Christianity (the main religious tradition in Britain) differs from Islam in terms of the way Christians pray.

The development of this idea successfully identifies what is different in Christianity – in this case, that men and women pray together.

The student answer shows knowledge of worship in Islam and states the method Muslims use when praying.

In the second part of this answer, the student correctly identifies that Muslim men and women pray in different rooms. The reason for this is stated but it is not needed to answer the question.

67

Answers

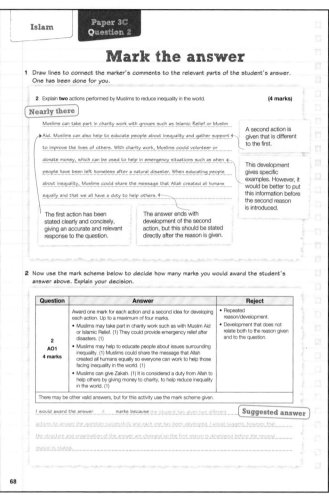

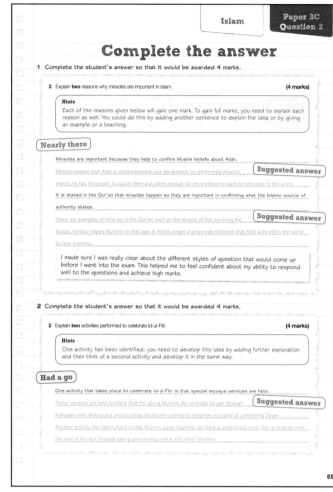

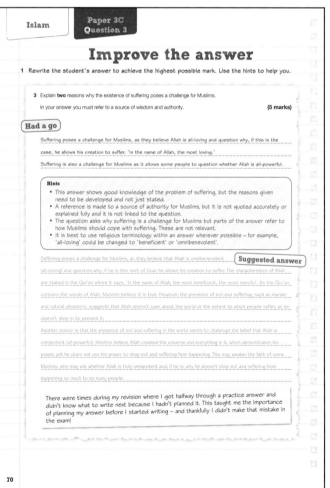

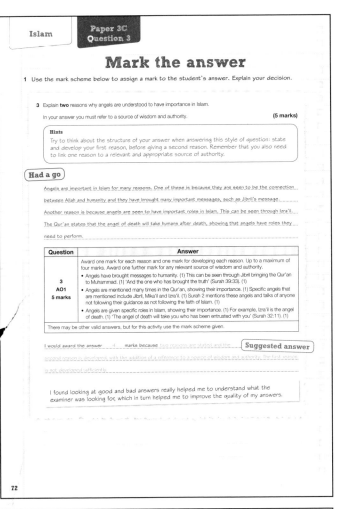

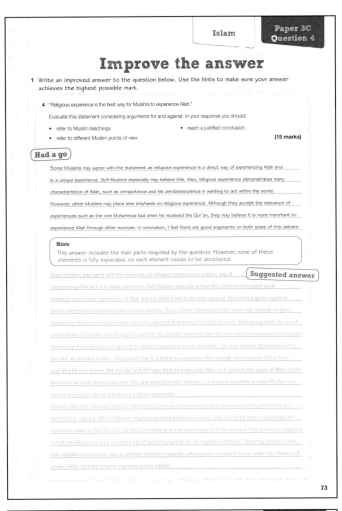

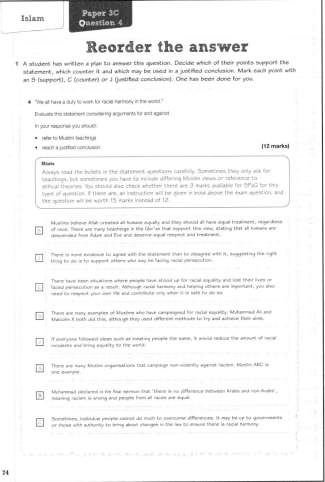

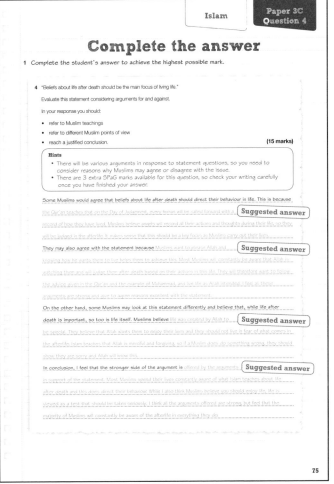

Published by Pearson Education Limited, 80 Strand, London, WC2R 0RL.

www.pearsonschoolsandfecolleges.co.uk

Copies of official specifications for all Pearson qualifications may be found on the website: qualifications.pearson.com

Text and illustrations © Pearson Education Ltd 2019
Typeset by Newgen KnowledgeWorks Pvt. Ltd., Chennai, India
Produced by Newgen Publishing UK
Cover illustration by Eoin Coveney

The right of Tanya Hill to be identified as author of this work has been asserted by her in accordance with the Copyright, Designs and Patents Act 1988.

First published 2019

22 21 20 19
10 9 8 7 6 5 4 3 2 1

British Library Cataloguing in Publication Data
A catalogue record for this book is available from the British Library

ISBN 978 1 292 29667 8

Acknowledgements
We would like to thank Joni Sommerville, Theo Mellors, Emily Plenty, John-Paul Duddy, Emily Atkinson, Jess Salmon, Holly Coop, Matthew Foot and David Birch for their invaluable help in providing student tips for the series.

Non-prominent Text Credits:
P 4, 10, 28, 34, 36, 38, 60, 76–78, 82–84, 89–90: Biblica, Inc.: THE HOLY BIBLE, NEW INTERNATIONAL VERSION®, NIV® Copyright © 1973, 1978, 1984, 2011 by Biblica, Inc.™ Used by permission. All rights reserved worldwide; **P 24, 46–47, 72, 81, 85, 86, 91, 93: The Qur'an Project Distribution Centre:** 'The Qur'an Project (Saheeh International Translation), Maktabah Booksellers and Publishers (2010).

Notes from the publisher
1. While the publishers have made every attempt to ensure that advice on the qualification and its assessment is accurate, the official specification and associated assessment guidance materials are the only authoritative source of information and should always be referred to for definitive guidance.

Pearson examiners have not contributed to any sections in this resource relevant to examination papers for which they have responsibility.

2. Pearson has robust editorial processes, including answer and fact checks, to ensure the accuracy of the content in this publication, and every effort is made to ensure this publication is free of errors. We are, however, only human, and occasionally errors do occur. Pearson is not liable for any misunderstandings that arise as a result of errors in this publication, but it is our priority to ensure that the content is accurate. If you spot an error, please do contact us at resourcescorrections@pearson.com so we can make sure it is corrected.